Running from Office

RUNNING FROM OFFICE

Why Young Americans Are Turned Off to Politics

JENNIFER L. LAWLESS

and

RICHARD L. FOX

OXFORD
UNIVERSITY PRESS

OXFORD
UNIVERSITY PRESS

Oxford University Press is a department of the University of Oxford.
It furthers the University's objective of excellence in research, scholarship,
and education by publishing worldwide.

Oxford   New York
Auckland   Cape Town   Dar es Salaam   Hong Kong   Karachi
Kuala Lumpur   Madrid   Melbourne   Mexico City   Nairobi
New Delhi   Shanghai   Taipei   Toronto

With offices in
Argentina   Austria   Brazil   Chile   Czech Republic   France   Greece
Guatemala   Hungary   Italy   Japan   Poland   Portugal   Singapore
South Korea   Switzerland   Thailand   Turkey   Ukraine   Vietnam

Oxford is a registered trade mark of Oxford University Press
in the UK and certain other countries.

Published in the United States of America by
Oxford University Press
198 Madison Avenue, New York, NY 10016

© Oxford University Press 2015

Library of Congress Cataloging-in-Publication Data
Lawless, Jennifer L., 1975–
  Running from office : why young Americans are turned off to politics / Jennifer
L. Lawless and Richard L. Fox.
    p. cm.
  ISBN 978–0–19–939765–5 (hardback) 1. Young adults—Political activity—United
States. 2. Young adults—United States—Attitudes. 3. Students—Political activity—
United States. 4. Students—United States—Attitudes. 5. Political participation—
United States. 6. Political culture—United States. I. Fox, Richard Logan. II. Title.
  HQ799.9.P6L38 2015
  320.408350973—dc23
                              2014039232

9   8   7   6   5   4   3   2   1

Printed in the United States of America on acid-free paper

CONTENTS

LIST OF FIGURES

LIST OF TABLES

For nearly 20 years, we have worked together to understand why so few women hold elective office in the United States. And it's been a fun ride (more on that later). The main argument we've made is that women are less politically ambitious than men. They're less likely to think about running for office, less likely to be recruited to run, less likely to think they're qualified to run, and less likely actually to throw their hats into the ring. These gender differences, we've argued, are deeply embedded and fully intact by the time women and men enter the professions from which most political candidates emerge. When we initially embarked on the project that would serve as the basis for this book, we expected to stay on our usual path. We would survey and interview thousands of high school and college students and try to determine the origins of the gender gap in political ambition.

But a funny thing happened on the way to the data set. In May 2012, we were sitting in a hotel lobby, designing our national survey about young people's political ambition, when one of our cellphones buzzed. A reporter from *Inside Higher Education* wanted to know if we cared to respond to Congressman (now Senator) Jeff Flake's comments about defunding the National Science Foundation's Political Science program. Why was the reporter calling us, we wondered? And then it became clear. Ours—the project we were working on at that moment—was among those singled out by Representative Flake as frivolous research that "might satisfy the curiosities of a few academics," but carry no broader benefit to society. From the floor of the House, Flake had asked incredulously about the funds set aside to "study gender and political ambition among high school and college students? That's what we're paying for here . . . How can we justify this outcome?"

As Congressman Flake condemned this research, congressional approval was at an all-time low, legislative gridlock and partisan posturing were at all-time highs, and the debt ceiling, immigration reform, and climate change were among the important issues Congress repeatedly failed to address. The political system was widely perceived as broken, and for good reason. Yet here was Congressman Flake, saying that it was not important to understand how young people felt about their government or whether they aspired to be a part of it. In many ways, the congressman's behavior embodied why young people don't want to run for office. We quipped to the *Higher Ed* reporter, "We may no longer need to conduct the study. This gives us plenty of evidence."

As we ended the call and returned to designing the survey, we were reminded of the many conversations we'd had with each other, our colleagues, and our students about the unappealing nature of contemporary politics. Given hyperpartisanship, legislative gridlock, a never-ending array of political scandals, and an unforgiving 24-hour news cycle, why would any young person—male or female—possibly be interested in running for office? Contemporary politicians give young people plenty of reason to become either completely disengaged or downright disgusted. Although exploring the origins of the gender gap in political ambition is important, we quickly came to realize that the more immediate crisis in need of investigation was whether, and if so, how, today's political system and its leaders have turned off an entire generation.

And that's what we offer in the pages that follow. Our surveys and interviews with thousands of high school and college students make it clear that the overwhelming majority of young people have no interest in running for office. They'd rather do almost anything else. Young people who want to be leaders, improve their communities, or make the world a better place do not think twice before dismissing electoral office as a viable path. They view the political system as ineffective, broken, and unappealing. But we do more than demonstrate how contemporary politics sucks the political lifeblood out of young people. We also offer a set of recommendations that we believe can help steer a new course. There are more than 500,000 elective offices in the United States. We need to make sure that the best and the brightest young people aspire to hold them.

As is often the case, coming up with the idea, justifying the inquiry, and crafting the central argument are the easy parts; the mechanics of actually writing the book are more difficult. Indeed, anyone who knows us knows that it has been a long 20 years of coauthorship, much akin to a highly dysfunctional yet codependent marriage. This is not to say that there haven't been lots of ups. Completing several books, publishing many articles, and realizing that people are still willing to respond to surveys have provided moments of celebration and relief. But we're pretty familiar with the downs, too. The raging arguments, manic episodes, slammed phones, snippy texts, and passive-aggressive emails have, naturally, tested our resolve from time to time. We are happy to report, however, that the execution of this project was smoother than much of our earlier work. Only once in writing this book, for instance, did someone try to quit the project. Only three times did we actually stop speaking to each other. The number of two-hour, tear-filled, soul-crushing phone conversations can be counted on two hands and one foot. And the number of ad hominem attacks is in the dozens, not the hundreds. By our standards, this book is a triumph of collaboration and personal growth.

It is also a product of the help and support of many colleagues and friends. We must begin by thanking Danny Hayes and Sean Theriault. Although they would have made it into the acknowledgments simply for providing feedback on our original proposal to the National Science Foundation (NSF), commenting on multiple versions of the survey, and acting as willing sounding boards for all of our ideas as we drafted the book, both were overachievers. They each took with them on vacation a draft of the full manuscript so that they could read it and respond in a timeframe that worked for us. Their careful and insightful comments improved the book immeasurably, both in substance and style.

We are also grateful to many people who provided feedback on the NSF proposal and survey, and who read parts of the manuscript: Kathy Dolan, Samantha Hay, Andrew Healy, Kent Jennings, Jan Leighley, Zoe Oxley, Kathryn Pearson, Sue Tolleson-Rinehart, Wendy Schiller, Matt Wright, and very engaged seminar participants at Duke University, Brigham Young University, and the Kennedy School of Government. Many of our colleagues happily allowed us to bounce ideas off of them, so we thank Andrew Dilts, Michael Genovese, John Parrish, Jennifer Ramos, Jim Thurber, and Antoine Yoshinaka. And we appreciate that Adriana DiPasquale and Ben Gray were willing to read the first chapter and assess whether "regular people" would be at all interested in what we have to say and how we say it.

When Gail Baitinger and Samantha Guthrie agreed to help us conduct hour-long phone interviews with more than 100 of our survey respondents, they probably did not realize that they'd be spending the summer of 2013 on the phone with teenagers who would rather be doing pretty much anything else. Gail and Sam persevered, though, and were far more effective than we were at drawing out young people's attitudes about government, politics, and political ambition. Because of their efforts, the book is richer, more readable, and more interesting. Although it would take pages to itemize all of the other tasks they completed, suffice it to say that no other graduate students will ever compare. Gail even copyedited the final version of the manuscript in record time. (All errors are hers, not ours!)

From a practical standpoint, we also have many people to thank. Our endeavor would have been impossible without financial support from the National Science Foundation, which funded the survey of high school and college students, and the Women & Politics Institute at American University, which paid for the follow-up interviews. Joe Garrett and Sergei Rodkin at GfK Custom Research ensured that executing the survey and collecting the data were smooth sailing. Bill Brown, Matt Bourdon, and Rachel Pentlarge at American University, and Joseph McNicholas and his team at Loyola Marymount University, helped us navigate the world of federal grants. And Angela Chnapko, our editor at Oxford University Press, was supportive of the project from its inception. Her feedback played a vital role in developing the book's content, and the speed with which she moved the process along made her a pleasure to work with.

We are deeply indebted to the staff at the Women & Politics Institute. Not only did they endure daily updates about the progress of the book, but they also provided help and support every step of the way (from preparing the initial grant application to scanning the final page proofs). In particular, My-Lien Le handled seemingly endless administrative and bureaucratic annoyances with far more patience and competence than either of us could muster. She also, once again, very swiftly constructed a user-friendly index (and she indulged all of our needless questions throughout the process). Diane Hsiung took on every random task we could imagine, often at a moment's notice.

We would be remiss not to thank the more than 4,000 young people who participated in our survey and interviews. In many ways, this book is really written for them. We hope that their stories will make clear to politicians the long-term, dire implications of their behavior. We also hope that their words and the suggestions those words inspire will ultimately change how future generations think about running for office.

Finally, we'd like to thank our families and friends for enduring all that was entailed in our writing another book together. Many thought we were crazy to go down that path again. We hope we proved them wrong.

Running from Office

1

Coming of Age in an Era of Political
Dysfunction and Disillusionment

Aliza, an 18-year-old honors student from Cincinnati, Ohio, lives
in what she considers a "pretty liberal and pretty political" household.[1] Her mother constantly talks about politics, and the car
radio is always turned to NPR. For as long as she can remember,
Aliza's parents told her that "improving the world should be a
big priority." Armed with a passion for protecting the environment and a sense that politics is a way to "solve problems to make
things better," she volunteered for the Obama campaign in the
summer of 2012. Rather than feed her passion for change, though,
the campaign quickly soured Aliza to politics and government.
"Politics," she told us, "is just about getting votes. No one cares
about issues. No one cares about policy." As she prepares to head
off to college next fall, Aliza's interest in the environment remains
intact. But a career in politics is off the table: "I'm pretty sure that
whatever I do, I won't run for office. I'd hate to live my life like
that, the way people act in politics. I'd hate to sell out, especially
to accomplish so little."

Stacy lives in West Virginia and is a well-rounded 10th grader.
She loves sports and is a member of her school's volleyball,

basketball, and track-and-field teams. She also spends several hours every week volunteering in the community. Like Aliza, Stacy hopes to "improve the world" and "make the community a better place." She describes her home state as "pretty rough in some parts" and recognizes—through her volunteer work—that "there's a ton of poverty all around this area. There's no reason for that." We asked Stacy if she ever thought that running for office and becoming an elected leader might be a way she could improve her surroundings. She scoffed at the idea and went on to explain that her father, who considers himself a member of the Tea Party, has no respect for politics: "My Dad hates the government and he hates the president. He always tells us how pointless it all is." Stacy has already developed a distaste for politics, too. "Elections," she explained, "are nasty with the candidates firing back at each other and making up stuff. And the politicians are only out for themselves . . . Based on what I've seen and what I've heard, I would never want to be in politics." Stacy believes that she can make the most positive change in her community by becoming a school counselor or an elementary school teacher.

Peter, a sophomore at a West Coast school, entered college planning to major in political science or public policy. In high school, he was on the debate team and "always loved talking about politics, current events, and what was going on in the world" with his teammates and friends. But during his first year of college, Peter started to lose his passion for politics: "I began to see how bad the system is. Whatever I'd watch on TV, whatever I'd see on the Internet, it was all so discouraging." He described a system where "politicians constantly lie," "stick with their party no matter what," and "don't seem to care about fairness or what's in the best interest of the country." Upon reflection, Peter remarked, "I started out as a kid who wanted to be president. Now, I am just as cynical about government as everyone else. I don't want to spend my time with that anymore." He told us that he will probably major in accounting and eventually pursue an MBA.

Terry imagines a career that will allow him to showcase his creativity. He is an excellent artist, so, as he begins to think about graduating from high school and applying to college, graphic design and architecture appeal to him as majors. Terry's family "almost never talks about politics." He does not know for whom— or even whether—his parents voted in the 2012 presidential election. But he is pretty sure that his father is a Republican. Despite his apolitical upbringing, Terry has a sense of what politics and campaigns are like: "Politicians just lie and they won't compromise. The campaigns are really ugly. The people in Washington can't seem to get anything done." He did not follow the 2012 election closely because he "had better things to do than watch Romney, who was, like, clueless and elitist, fight with Obama, who is trying to ruin the country." When we asked whether any circumstances might lead him to run for office someday, Terry laughed. "Are you kidding?" he asked. "I hate politics. If I want to help people or something, I can do it another way."

A high-quality, well-functioning democracy demands that the next generation hears—and then heeds—a call to public service. And there are certainly many ways young people can respond to that call. Community organizing, promoting political awareness through social media, working for a socially conscious business, staging an economic boycott, or starting an NGO are only some of the various paths they can pursue to be engaged citizens. But running for office is a critical one, too. Elected officials craft, shape, and implement the laws that affect citizens now and for generations to come. In addition, with more than 500,000 elected positions in the United States, the political system can sustain itself and succeed only if a large number of citizens eventually throw their hats into the ring. Yet, as Aliza, Stacy, Peter, and Terry make clear—and as we argue in the pages that follow—Washington's dreadful performance over the past two decades has taken a toll on the young Americans who have come to know politics through this spectacle. They see politics as pointless and unpleasant. They see political leaders as corrupt and selfish. They have no interest in entering the political arena. Ever.

We are not the first people to recognize the consequences of what is now widely perceived as a dysfunctional political system. Several recent books catalog the failures of government in the contemporary era. In *The Parties Versus the People*, former Republican Congressman Mickey Edwards laments how US politics has devolved into policy gridlock and partisan tribalism. Journalist E.J. Dionne's update to his classic book, *Why Americans Hate Politics*, argues that, as a result of a political system that values partisan power more than good ideas and common-ground solutions, the public feels deeply alienated. Thomas Mann and Norman Ornstein, two veteran congressional observers, arrive at a similar conclusion. Their book, *It's Even Worse than it Looks: How the American Constitutional System Collided with the New Politics of Extremism*, chronicles what they consider the most reckless and dysfunctional government they have seen during their 40 years in Washington, DC. These are just a few recent treatments of the broad implications of American gridlock and a broken political system.[2]

But we call attention to a devastating and completely overlooked consequence of political dysfunction: its effect on future generations' ambition to run for office. When our elected officials cheer failed policies, shut down the government, stymie political appointments, accuse their opponents of trying to destroy the country, and refuse to compromise, they engage in more than hyperbole and hyperpartisanship. They do more than generate policy stalemates and legislative gridlock. They damage more than the public's short-term political trust and confidence.

The mean-spirited, broken system that has come to characterize American politics turns young people off to the idea of running for office. It discourages them from aspiring, one day, to be elected leaders. It prevents them from even thinking about a career in politics.

We arrive at this conclusion by relying on an original, national survey we conducted of more than 4,000 high school and college students. In addition to the survey, we spoke at length with more than 100 of these young people about their political attitudes, life goals, personality traits, media habits, hobbies and interests, and family backgrounds. We integrate the stories of the people we interviewed with our national survey results to paint a political profile of the next generation that should sound alarm bells about the long-term, deeply embedded damage contemporary politics has wrought on US democracy and its youngest citizens. But our message is not one of only gloom and doom. Fortunately, the young women and men we surveyed and interviewed also provided some guidance for how to steer a new course, and it is in that direction forward that we conclude the book.

Growing Up in a Time of Partisan Warfare and Political Gridlock

Early in his memoir, former President Bill Clinton writes that he developed a clear sense of political ambition as a teenager: "Sometime in my sixteenth year I decided I wanted to be in public life as an elected official . . . I knew I could be great in public service."[3] Newt Gingrich, who served as Speaker of the U.S. House of Representatives from 1995 to 1999, began his life in politics by walking into City Hall in his hometown when he was just 12 years old. He thought the town needed a zoo, and he realized that he could "be a leader" in the effort.[4] Beau Biden, the attorney general of Delaware and son of Vice President Joe Biden, recalls, "You couldn't leave my dinner table without the sense that you had an obligation . . . to try to impact your world. . . . Eating was almost incidental to the discussion."[5]

Although political figures such as Clinton, Gingrich, and Biden might be unusual in the levels of electoral office they sought and success they achieved, their stories illustrate the powerful effects that political ambition early in life can have on an individual's career path. In fact, young people's initial career goals tend to be excellent predictors of the jobs they eventually get. Over the course of the last 20 years, researchers have tracked high school and college students' professional aspirations with the careers they ultimately pursue. These studies reveal a strong correlation between specific job aspirations at age 16 with those attained by age 35.[6] In our studies of adult potential candidates, we also uncovered a strong relationship between early thoughts of a candidacy and political ambition later in life. Nearly half of the lawyers, business leaders, educators, and political activists we surveyed who had considered running for office reported that the thought first occurred to them by the time they were in college. A general interest in, or openness toward, running for office early in life often sets the stage for a political candidacy decades later.

That's why we argue that contemporary American politics leaves the future of American democracy on precarious footing. Today's high school and college students have grown up knowing nothing other than a politics characterized by nasty campaigns, partisan posturing, a media establishment focused on conflict and scandal, and political pundits who perpetually stoke the flames of public anger and dismay.[7] This is not the kind of environment conducive to fostering or nurturing thoughts of a political candidacy later in life. In making this argument, we do not necessarily suggest that the current political climate is more rancorous, hopeless, or ineffective than it was in previous eras in US political history. Certainly, the Civil War, legislative battles during the civil rights movement, US involvement in Vietnam, and impeachment proceedings against two presidents (not to mention the forced resignation of another), are only a handful among the litany of political battles Americans have witnessed over time. We leave it to historians and other political scientists to determine where on the divisive and dysfunctional continuum today's politics falls. But we feel confident asserting that the current political system—the only one to which today's high school and college students have ever been exposed—is broken. And the digital era and 24-hour news cycle that characterize today's media landscape only heighten Americans' opportunities to access the most negative aspects of political news and reinforce their negative perceptions.

Chronicles of a Broken Political System

From the start, it is important to recognize that people tend to evaluate government and politics through a national lens. For many citizens, what happens in Washington, DC, shapes how they see all levels of politics and government. Scholars have shown that presidential scandals, tumultuous social, economic, and political times, and reactions to national political leaders directly influence citizens' trust in and cynicism toward government.[8] These events do more than affect presidential and congressional approval ratings, though. They also shape attitudes toward state and local governments.[9] This national lens is vital for our purposes in light of what the average American sees when perusing the paper, surfing the Internet, or flipping through the channels.

Media headlines typically and cynically pronounce the failures of the political system as business as usual. The government shutdown in fall 2013 serves as just one recent example. From furloughed workers to disgruntled tourists turned away from national parks, many Americans experienced firsthand the consequences of Washington politicians' inability to pass a federal budget. They also experienced around-the-clock news coverage that highlighted elected leaders' worst motives and characteristics. The *New York Daily News*, on the first day of the shutdown, ran the headline "House of Turds" over a picture of House Speaker John Boehner. The subtitles read: "D.C. Cess-Pols Shut Down the Government" and "They Get Paid While Nation Suffers."[10] The *Washington Post* went with, "In Shutdown Blame Game, Democrats and Republicans United: It's the Other Side's Fault."[11] (The *Post's* Style section cover was a bit more dramatic: a darkened Capitol building overlaid with the word "Ugh.") On day three of the crisis, *NBC Nightly News* anchor Brian Williams commented toward the end of the broadcast:

> Here tonight, it's been another eventful day in this country, certainly in our nation's capital and against the already dim backdrop of this government shutdown and the open partisan warfare. . . . All of it feeding into Americans' growing general uneasiness about what's happening in this place where they're supposed to be running things. At times it seems like things are coming apart a bit.[12]

When the government reopened 16 days later, a debate about raising the US debt ceiling commenced immediately. *CNN.com's* homepage flashed: "The biggest threat to the U.S. economy? Washington dysfunction."[13]

Assessments like these are now standard practice in how professional journalists and pundits describe national politics. Our LexisNexis search of major newspapers and broadcast news transcripts for 2013 returned routine mentions of the terms "partisan bickering" (472 news stories), "partisan warfare" (412 news stories), and "Washington dysfunction" (344 news stories). And these derisive descriptors do not even begin to approach the negativity and condemnation that characterize US politics in the blogosphere or on talk radio. As Matthew Kerbel and Joel David Bloom write, "If the Internet is still the Wild West of mass media, blogs are a territory where essentially anything goes, as people are free to post the most trivial, ridiculous, and fantastic ideas in frank language that would never be permitted on network television."[14] Indeed, a Google Blog search of the term "partisan bickering" for 2013 turned up more than 16,000 posts.

Political analysts often trace the current period of dysfunction to the modern Republican Party's attempts to run against the government in Washington. Iconic of this strategy was a 1986 press conference at which President Ronald Reagan asserted that "the nine most terrifying words in the English language are: I'm from the government and I'm here to help."[15] The assault on government ramped up considerably with the midterm elections of 1994. According to Thomas Mann and Norman Ornstein, Newt Gingrich recruited anti-Washington candidates who were willing to consider the White House, as well as their Democratic colleagues, mortal enemies. Thus, when voters gave Republicans control of the US House of Representatives for the first time in 40 years and Newt Gingrich ascended to Speaker of the House, he had a loyal GOP conference that not only shared his desire to slash the size of the federal government, but also supported his confrontational style. Gingrich's approach led to repeated showdowns with Democratic President Bill Clinton and ultimately resulted in two government shutdowns, one in late 1995 and the other in early 1996.

Since then, partisan wars have become the norm. In 1998, the Republicans launched a largely single-party attempt to impeach

Bill Clinton for lying about his affair with White House intern Monica Lewinsky. Two years later, the dispute over the outcome of the 2000 presidential election between Democratic Vice President Al Gore and Republican Governor George W. Bush saw its way to the US Supreme Court, where the justices decided the case along party lines. The events of September 11, 2001, provided a short-lived hiatus from the divisive partisanship that plagued the first eight months of the Bush administration; Democrats and Republicans even joined together for a congressional rendition of "God Bless America" on the steps of the Capitol. But bipartisan cooperation quickly disappeared. Almost immediately after the 2003 invasion of Iraq, Democrats accused President Bush and the Republicans of lying about the presence of weapons of mass destruction to justify the war. By the 2006 midterm elections, Democrats in districts all across the country campaigned on a promise to hold George Bush and the Republicans in Washington accountable for their actions.

Barack Obama's 2008 presidential campaign promised to change the way Washington did business. Yet from the earliest moments of the Obama administration, partisan battles continued to dominate US politics. Republicans gathered the evening before the inauguration and vowed to fight all Obama initiatives from the minute he took office.[16] And they were steadfast in their commitment. The president could count on very little Republican support as he pushed through an economic stimulus package; and virtually no Republicans supported Obama's signature health care reform. In fact, Senate Republicans used parliamentary tactics to stall or kill almost the entire Democratic agenda—from health care to energy to climate change to domestic spending.[17] In the words of then-Senate Minority Leader Mitch McConnell, "The single most important thing we want to achieve is for President Obama to be a one-term president."[18]

When the Republicans won back the House of Representatives in 2010, the situation only worsened. The GOP regained control, in large part, because of the success of Tea Party candidates, most of whom campaigned against government and many of whom demonstrated no interest in the type of political compromise that a two-party system demands.[19] Accordingly, the parties have been at loggerheads over almost every policy and have taken the country through three debt ceiling debates that imperiled the federal government's credit rating and a government shutdown that furloughed thousands of workers. A 2013 *Congressional Quarterly* study of voting patterns in the House and Senate revealed the highest levels of partisan voting in the history of the US Congress.[20] A *National Journal* study identified the 113th Congress as the most polarized since they started measuring the phenomenon in 1982.[21]

Evidence from the Polls: The Loss of Political Trust, Confidence, and Approval

Not surprisingly, the political climate of the last 20 years has culminated in the most negative public attitudes toward government since the advent of modern polling. The Pew Research Center, which began tracking public trust in the government in 1958, has uncovered a steady downward trend. By 2013, not even one in five voters trusted government to do what is right at least most of the time (see Figure 1.1). Approval ratings for Congress, which generally signal how citizens feel about the national government, are also in deep decline. Gallup recorded a congressional approval rating of just 9 percent in November 2013. In the past five years, no less than six prominent polling agencies— Gallup, CBS/*New York Times*, NBC/*Wall Street Journal*, Quinnipiac, ABC News/*Washington Post*, and Pew—have reported record lows for congressional approval. Upon the release of one such poll in 2011, US Senator John McCain joked that Congress is down to "paid staffers and blood relatives" approving of the job they do.[22]

Figure 1.1 Trust in the Federal Government and Congressional Approval, 2002—2014

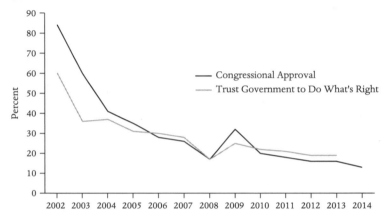

Notes: Data indicate respondents' responses to the following questions: "Do you approve or disapprove of the way Congress is handling its job?" and "How much of the time do you think you can trust government in Washington to do what is right—just about always, most of the time, or only some of the time?" Congressional approval data are from Gallup; government trust data are from the PEW Research Center for the People & the Press, and combine "just about always" and "most of the time" responses.

Senator McCain's quip is not far off the mark. In early 2013, Public Policy Polling conducted a survey that asked respondents whether they had a more favorable impression of the US Congress or of someone or something else that is generally unpopular. The results of these 26 head-to-head matchups, while amusing, demonstrate the low regard most Americans have for members of Congress. Citizens rated root canals, traffic jams, cockroaches, and used-car salesmen higher than they did members of Congress (See Table 1.1).

Table 1.1 Ranking of Congress Compared to Other Unpopular People, Institutions, and Circumstances

What do you have a higher opinion of: Congress or . . .	
	Margin
Rank higher than Congress:	
Lice	+48%
Brussels sprouts	+46
Colonoscopies	+27
Used-car salesmen	+25
Root canals	+24
Traffic jams	+22
NFL replacement refs	+17
France	+9
Carnies	+8
Nickelback	+7
Genghis Khan	+4
Washington, DC political pundits	+3
Cockroaches	+2
Donald Trump	+2
Rank lower than Congress:	
Lindsay Lohan	−4
Playground bullies	−5
Telemarketers	−10
The Kardashians	−13
John Edwards	−16
Lobbyists	−18
Fidel Castro	−22
Gonorrhea	−25
Ebola	−28
Communism	−34
North Korea	−35
Meth labs	−39

Notes: Data are from a Public Policy Polling survey of 830 registered voters (conducted January 3–6, 2013). Each entry reports the net difference in a head-to-head matchup between Congress and the entity in question. Positive scores indicate higher relative popularity than Congress; negative entries indicate that Congress was perceived as more popular.

Members of the House and Senate might take solace in knowing that they rated more highly than playground bullies, telemarketers, North Korea, and meth labs. Or maybe not; in several cases, the margin was close.

Examining attitudes beyond trust in government and congressional approval further reveals the public's negative perceptions of contemporary politics. By late 2013, gridlock in Washington and the rocky rollout of the Affordable Care Act resulted in less than one in seven Americans expressing satisfaction with the way government functioned.[23] The polling data also make it clear that citizens were not only disgusted with political institutions; they had also had it with their own representatives. For decades, pollsters found that, while voters generally expressed high levels of discontent with Congress overall, they tended to approve of their own members. That ironclad reality was turned on its head in 2013, when 60 percent of voters favored replacing the entire Congress, including their own incumbent (see Table 1.2). Roughly half believed that "if members of Congress were replaced with random people walking down the street," those everyday Americans could do a better job handling the country's problems.[24] Public condemnation toward the political system could not be much more complete.

The young women and men who came of age or first experienced politics during these times of political disillusionment are certainly susceptible to these trends. Barack Obama's 2008 presidential campaign provided a rare moment of inspiration for many Americans, particularly young people, to believe in the possibility of unifying and repairing the political establishment in Washington. The campaign promise worked. Obama won the election in part because he received 66 percent of the votes of people under the age of 30, the highest percentage since exit polling recorded age-based breakdowns of vote choice.[25] But executing that promise posed more difficulties than the campaign envisioned. And many who began with high hopes for the Obama presidency have since become disillusioned. By the fall of 2014, support for President Obama among 18–29 year olds had sunk to 43 percent, which placed young voters in line with older voters.[26]

Table 1.2 Public Attitudes toward Politicians

On the whole, are you satisfied with the way the nation is being governed?		
	Satisfied	14%
	Dissatisfied	83
What is your opinion of the members of the US Congress?		
	High or Very High	8
	Low or Very Low	66
If there were a place on the ballot that allowed you to vote to defeat and replace every single member of Congress, including your own representative, would you?		
	Yes	60
	No	35
To get a fresh start in Washington, are you ready to vote out of office your own senators and congressional representative?		
	Yes	72
	No	23
If members of Congress were replaced with random people walking down the street, do you think those everyday Americans could do a better job handling the country's problems than Congress?		
	Yes	46
	No	47

Notes: Data are drawn from polls conducted by Fox News (October 20–22, 2013), NBC News/*Wall Street Journal* (October 7–9, 2013), CNN/ORC (October 18–20, 2013), and Gallup (December 5–8, 2013).

A *USA Today*/Pew survey found that only four in ten young voters approved of the president's signature health care law (40 percent of voters over the age of 30 also approved of the measure).[27] According to John Della Volpe, polling director at Harvard University's Institute of Politics, "Young Americans hold the president, Congress, and the federal government in less esteem almost by the day, and the levels of engagement they are having in politics are also on the decline."[28]

Turned Off to Politics: The Rest of the Book

Academics, politicians, political practitioners, and commentators agree that it is important for young people to be politically engaged. Widespread efforts to heighten civic engagement among high school and college students have become a mainstay of American politics. The Circle Foundation, for example, has devoted millions of dollars to conducting, funding, and evaluating research on the relationship between civic education and young Americans' civic engagement.[29] Rock the Vote, founded in 1990 and active in all presidential election campaigns since 1992, uses "music, popular culture, new technologies and grassroots organizing to motivate and mobilize young people in our country to participate in every election, with the goal of seizing the power of the youth vote to create political and social change."[30] And voter registration drives, campaign rallies, and volunteer opportunities are abundant on college campuses every election season.

There is also no shortage of academic research that examines young people's interest in politics. For the past several decades, researchers have examined low levels of youth political engagement, lamented the problem, and attributed it to several factors. Some suggest that there are no great issues of the day to motivate the interest and participation that accompanied the Cold War or the

Vietnam War draft.[31] Others argue that the digital generation has induced young people into a self-indulgent social-media haze.[32] Still others make the case that the educational system has not successfully imbued a sense of civic duty in young people.[33] Some scholars even suggest that the seeming lack of interest is a byproduct of new forms of activism that are horizontal, transnational, and less dependent on money. Even though young people might not vote or engage in conventional acts of participation at the same rates as older adults, for example, Russell Dalton argues that the younger generation is more engaged, more tolerant, and more supportive of social justice. Lance Bennett suggests that young people do not consider the nation-state a particularly important political venue, so they strive to be good citizens not through conventional electoral politics, but, rather, through new forms of activism.

Regardless of the underlying reasons, most warn of the deleterious consequences of a democracy where young people do not care about government or the traditional ways to engage the governing process. David Mindich's *Tuned Out: Why Americans Under 40 Don't Follow the News*, for instance, focuses on young citizens' declining interest in current events and news. His prognostications, based on a series of interviews, are dire. He worries about the fate of a democracy in which so few people actually know what is going on in the world around them. Political scientist Martin Wattenberg's *Is Voting for Young People?* documents the decline in young people's political activism and warns of younger generations' underrepresentation in the political system. Aaron Martin sounds a similar note in *Young People and Politics: Political Engagement in the Anglo-American Democracies*, arguing that youth political engagement is quite limited in the United States, as well as across a number of Western democracies. And Henry Milner's *The Internet Generation: Engaged Citizens or Political Dropouts* provides a cautionary tale about how technology affects young people's political engagement and the consequences for sustaining democratic governments around the world.

Yet despite nonprofit organizations that focus on youth civic engagement and academic accounts of young people's political activism, we know little about their political ambition. We have not examined how today's nasty and polarized political environment affects young people's willingness or aspirations to run for office. We are left to wonder whether the next generation will fulfill a call to public service by entering the electoral arena.[34]

This book changes that. We provide an authoritative account of young people's political ambition and the factors that trigger and undermine it. Ultimately, we have three goals: (1) to document high school and college students' low levels of interest in running for office; (2) to explain how their lack of political ambition is linked to contemporary politics; and (3) to highlight the factors that can propel young people's ambition even in this dysfunctional environment. In our attempt to raise concerns about a political process that systematically alienates future generations of potential leaders from contemplating a political career, we divide the remainder of the book into five chapters.

Chapter 2 establishes the crux of the problem: Our national survey of 2,163 high school students (ages 13 to 17) and 2,117 college students (ages 18 to 25) reveals that young people's career interests are broad and their desire to improve the world strong, but that politics is not a route they plan to pursue.[35] Regardless of how we ask the question or what scenario we present, the next generation conveys almost no interest in running for office. Although we uncover some important demographic differences in political ambition—to which we are attentive throughout the book—disinterest in running for office characterizes young people across the board: Black or white, rich or poor, liberal or conservative, northeastern or southern, the next generation is turned off to politics.

Chapters 3 – 5 rely on our survey results and interviews to explain why young people don't want to run for office. It is easy to blame American youth for their lack of civic engagement. We criticize them for being consumed by materialism, devoting their time to writing self-involved tweets and Facebook posts, and lacking intellectual curiosity and a thirst for information. While these criticisms are often valid, much of the blame also lies with a political system and its political figures. Indeed, the limited encounters young people have with politics—in their families, at school, with their friends, and through the media—impress upon them that political leaders are dishonest and self-interested, and that the political system is broken and ineffective. Beyond this exposure, young people's parents and teachers—their mentors and sources of inspiration—do not encourage them even to think about running for office. Of course, why would they? The very people who could influence young people's personal and professional aspirations and goals are turned off to politics themselves. As a result, very few of today's high school and college students have any aspirations to be political leaders. They don't receive the message that politics is a profession worth pursuing.

Chapter 6 concludes the book with a set of recommendations for how to encourage the next generation to consider running for office. We begin with a brief plea to contemporary politicians and pundits to think about how their conduct affects future generations. Because we understand that the plea will likely fall on deaf ears, the bulk of the chapter offers a series of specific actions that can be taken to spur young people to rise up and aspire to be elected leaders. Here, we circumvent the politicians, choosing instead to address parents, teachers, political organizations, philanthropists, and the media. Young people may be turned off to politics, but given the stakes, it's vital to turn them on.

2

What Do You Want To Be When You Grow Up? Not a Politician!

People in politics, they are squirrely. They say they're going to do something, but they don't do it. I don't want to be part of that.

—Charlotte, *high school junior from Texas*

I am going into farming. Politics is for people who like to bang their heads against the wall. I'd rather milk cows than run for office.

—Thornton, *college senior from New York*

By the time you're done with politics, your hair has turned grey. I want to keep my hair not grey. I don't even want to think about a career in politics.

—Franklin, *college sophomore from Iowa*

519,682. That's the number of elected officials in the United States. Several hundred serve at the federal level, in positions most of us know well: 535 are members of the US Congress, and the president and vice president govern from Pennsylvania Avenue. But an additional 7,382 citizens are state legislators. More than 1,000 others are elected to state boards, such as the Public Utilities Commission in South Dakota, the Public Service Commission in Tennessee, the Railroad Commission in Texas, and the Commission of Public Lands in New Mexico. And literally hundreds of thousands of people serve as mayors, city and town councilors, school board members, parks commissioners, soil and water conservation

directors, coroners, auditors, sewage disposal authorities, tax col-
lectors, and recorders of deeds, to name just a handful of elective positions.[1] All told, for every 600 people living in the United
States, one is an elected official.

The sheer volume of elective positions in the United States
places two demands on citizens. First, it requires that they perse-
vere through what can sometimes be an onerous ballot on Election Day. In 2012, for example, voters in some California counties
had to make selections in more than 25 contests, from president
at the top of the ticket down to community college trustee at the
bottom. The 2014 elections required many Texas voters to choose
among candidates for 40 offices, including governor, probate judge,
member of the board of education, and county treasurer. Second,
and more important for our purposes, the large number of elective
positions necessitates that millions of engaged citizens rise up and
seek these offices.[2] Sometimes, the races are hotly contested, expen-
sive, partisan battles. Other times, they are low-cost, nonpartisan,
uncompetitive contests. But each requires at least one person—and
ideally more than that—in each election cycle to emerge as a candidate. Given that political ambition tends to form early in life, the
political system can flourish only if young people—the best and
the brightest of the next generation—are eager to run for office.

But they're not. In this chapter, we turn to our national survey
of more than 4,200 high school and college students, as well as our
in-depth interviews with 115 of them. We demonstrate that most
would never consider running for office. The overwhelming majority express no interest in a future candidacy, be it at the local,
state, or federal level. And very few young women and men place
a political career anywhere on their list of professional aspirations.
Today's high school and college students would actually prefer to
do almost anything else. This is striking, given that most of the
young people we surveyed articulated a strong commitment to

serving their communities and improving the world. Ultimately, the results of our research raise questions about the future of democratic politics in the United States. They also set the stage for the remainder of the book, which delves into the reasons that young people are turned off to electoral politics and offers a serious indictment of today's political climate.

A National Survey of Young People's Ambition

Most 45-year-olds don't wake up one day, look in the mirror, and decide to run for public office. When people do decide to enter the fray, the idea has usually been in their heads and percolating for quite some time. Maybe they were not sure when they would run, or that the right opportunity would ever arise. Perhaps they did not know for certain what position they would seek. They probably had not fully considered the nuts and bolts of what a campaign might entail. But the seed of a potential candidacy was likely planted years ago, often dating back to childhood or young adulthood. Yet, scholars who study political ambition have not focused on young people.

Instead, the vast majority of research that investigates who runs for office concentrates on actual candidates and elected officials, or professionally established adults.[3] These studies, however, cannot tell us much about how contemporary politics affects political ambition. Consider research that focuses on members of Congress. In the 113th Congress (2012–2014), the average member of the US House of Representatives was 57 years old; only 8.5 percent of the members were younger than 40. The average US Senator was 62. The youngest (Chris Murphy, a Democrat from Connecticut) turned 41 in 2014.[4] The numbers are similar for state legislators: the average age is 56, and only 4 percent are younger than 35.[5] Even studies of potential candidates—men and women who have the educational and professional backgrounds common among politicians—contain hardly any respondents who are younger than 40.[6] This means that virtually none of these women and men grew up amid the gridlock and hyperpartisanship that characterize today's politics.

If we want to understand the relationships among early life experiences, the current political system, and political ambition, then we must survey and interview people at the time they begin to form their attitudes about running for office. And this is exactly what we did. Before turning to our national survey results, however, we must offer one caveat: We provide compelling evidence to show that today's high school and college students are not interested in running for office, and that much of their disinterest stems from their attitudes about contemporary politics. But we cannot directly compare the political ambition of young people today with that of previous generations. No one has ever before conducted a large, in-depth study of young people's political ambition, so we simply don't know whether they were more politically ambitious in the 1970s, 1980s, or 1990s. Wherever we can, we draw from public opinion polls and surveys from previous time periods to help place our findings in a broader context. And these data suggest that young people's political interest, exposure, and ambition are, in fact, lower now than in the past. But ultimately, we are most concerned with how today's politics has turned off the next generation of potential political leaders, and for this point, we have considerable evidence.

Anything but Politics: The Next Generation's Attitudes toward a Political Career

A national study of young Americans' political ambition allows us to address previously unanswered questions: Do young women and men aspire to be political leaders? Is the next generation ready to take the reins of political power? What backgrounds and characteristics differentiate young citizens who are politically ambitious from those who are not? Such an investigation is challenging, however, because thinking about an eventual political career is often very far removed from young people's daily lives. They interact with their family and friends. They go to school. They participate in extracurricular activities. They spend hours each day texting and online. They often work at least part-time. This does not mean that they do not also think about their future professional goals. But it does suggest that we need to be creative in measuring interest in a political career, which might not be first and foremost in young people's minds.

In order to examine interest in running for office, we developed several survey and interview questions. Some focus on general interest in running for office, whereas others ask about specific elective positions. Some ask our respondents to rank a series of professions, including politics, while others ask them to identify all of the career fields they might consider. Some ask for young people's gut reactions to the idea of running for office, and others ask them to elaborate on why it is something they would or would not like to do. In presenting and analyzing the results, we rely on our large national survey, as well as on the nuances and sentiments that came through in our interviews. Together, the responses paint a disturbing picture. It doesn't matter how we ask the question; today's high school and college students have very little interest in ever running for office.

Huh? and No Way! Initial Reactions to the Idea of Running for Office

Perhaps the best way to begin to document young people's lack of political ambition is with their responses to a general question we asked in the interviews: "Have you ever thought about running for office and becoming a political leader?" Most of the answers fall into one of two categories: befuddlement and derision.

For about one-quarter of the 115 high school and college students, our question was simply bizarre. The idea of running for office was far beyond anything that had ever crossed their minds, so they were not really sure how to answer. Often, the question was met with silence, followed by, "No." Other times, they responded like they were being thrown a question from out of left field. "Like in politics?" asked Cindy, a high school junior from California who hopes to become a teacher. "No. I've never thought about that." Mike, an English major at a large university in the South, reacted similarly: "Huh? . . . . What do you mean run for office? Like become the governor? No, that's not something that's ever occurred to me." Eva, a business major, offered a common response as well: "Uh . . . no. No one has ever asked me that before. But no, I would never run for office."

Most of the people we interviewed, however, were less perplexed by the question. For some of them, the idea of running had at least appeared on their radar screen at some point in time. It did not stay there long, though; these young women and men were very negative about the idea of entering politics. From their perceptions of how their families would react, to their attitudes toward how the political systems functions (or doesn't), to what they think about politicians, young people offered a litany of reasons why running for office does not appeal to them:

> If I ever told my parents I wanted to run for Congress, they would laugh at me. . . . They think politics is awful. I'd be crazy to want to do that. (Julius, high school senior)

I've thought about it and would never want to be president. Or have any political job. It sounds horrible. People hate you and are always on your case. (Nick, high school sophomore)

I don't think I would ever run for anything. My dad is in the army and he talks about politics and says things about how the country is in bad shape. He makes it sound too overwhelming to deal with. (Perris, high school freshman)

I don't think I'd run. Every time I turn on the news and politics comes on, it is just frustrating. I have pretty much stopped looking at any political headlines. News about politics sucks. (Carla, college junior)

There's so much that goes on behind the scenes that's not honest. I'd feel bad having to give into that behavior. I wouldn't want to do something immoral, or even illegal, to make a deal. (Deshauna, college senior)

For others, even though they had not previously given entering politics much thought, their visceral reactions led them to dismiss the idea right away:

Run for office? No way. Maybe some people think that being president is a romantic idea, but not me. (Amelia, college sophomore)

No way. I've never been interested in that kind of thing, that kind of negative atmosphere. (Adam, college sophomore)

No, never. When politics is discussed in my family it is a discussion about how terrible the president or the Congress is. Why would anyone want to do it? (Suzanne, college senior)

No! It's about lying, cheating, getting nothing done. That's not how I want to spend my time. (Todd, high school junior)

In almost every case, these reactions illustrate young people's negativity toward or disconnectedness from politics, the origins of which we explore in chapters 3, 4, and 5.

The 89 Percent: General Distaste toward Running for Office

Responses to our national survey corroborate what we found when conducting our interviews. Let's turn first to our most straightforward survey question about political ambition: "Have you ever thought that, someday, when you're older, you might want to run for a political office?" The top of Figure 2.1 presents responses to this question. Only about one out of every nine young citizens ever gave running for office any sort of serious thought. On the other hand, running for office never even crossed the minds of more than 60 percent of the high school and college students we surveyed.

The remaining 28 percent of respondents indicated that running for office had crossed their minds at least once. It became clear throughout the interviews, however, that these were not more than fleeting thoughts. Consider the exchange we had with John, a high school sophomore. When we asked John if he had ever considered running for office, he responded, "Uh . . . yeah, I guess." When we asked how often he considered it and the offices he was most interested in seeking, though, he said, "Oh, I have no idea. I guess I haven't really thought about it. I mean, I thought about it when you just asked." We had a similar conversation with Sarah, a college junior. She initially stated that running for office crossed her mind "a couple of times."

Figure 2.1 Young People's Interest in Running for Office

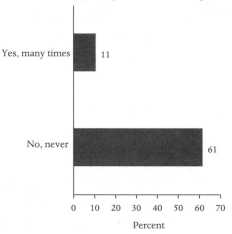

Have you ever thought that someday, when you're older,
you might want to run for a political office?

Percent

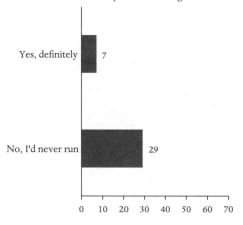

Even if you've never thought about it, could you
see yourself running for office one day?

Notes: N = 4,279. In the top panel, the remaining 28 percent of respondents indicated that running for office had crossed their minds at least once. In the bottom panel, the remainder of the respondents fell somewhere between "definitely" and "never." Most responded "probably not."

But as we began to ask follow-up questions, she told us that "it was not like a real thought or anything that would ever happen." Accordingly, here and throughout the book, we consider respondents to be politically ambitious if they have given running for office any semblance of serious thought.

We also asked them to tell us whether they could ever envision themselves running for office at some point in the future, even if they had never considered it. Here, too, the results reveal widespread disinterest. Only 7 percent reported that they plan to run for office at some point later in life. To put this number in perspective, roughly the same percentage of Americans report that they have personally witnessed an alien spaceship.[7] Six times as many teenagers and young adults have perfected the art of texting with their eyes closed.[8]

These low levels of political ambition transcend demographic and political characteristics. Regardless of sex, race, region, religion, party affiliation, income, or education, most young people do not want to run for office in the future. Certainly, there are some notable ambition differences among the people we surveyed. As we might expect, partisans—both Democrats and Republicans—are more than twice as likely as those who do not identify with a political label to report interest in running for office. And college students are two and a half times as likely as high school students to have considered a candidacy; as people get older and gain more exposure to a variety of professions, it follows that they will consider a broader array of career options (see Table 2.1).[9] The survey results also reveal that men are approximately 60 percent more likely than women to consider running for office, blacks and Latinos are about 44 percent more likely than whites to express political ambition, and Christian evangelicals are two-thirds more likely than respondents who identify with another religion or none at all to articulate interest in a political career.

Table 2.1 Young People's Interest in Running for Office, by Demographic Group

	Would Consider Running for Office in the Future
Sex	
Male	13% *
Female	8
Race	
White	9*
Black	12
Latino/Hispanic	13
Other	13
Religion	
Born-again Christian/Evangelical	15*
Other	9
Party Affiliation	
Democrat	14
Independent	12
Republican	11
Other or No political party affiliation	5
Estimated Household Income	
Less than $50,000	11
$50,000–$99,999	10
$100,000–$149,999	10
At least $150,000	11
Education	
Currently in high school	6*
Currently in college	15
N	4,280

Notes: Levels of significance: * indicates that the gap in political ambition is statistically significant at p < .05 within the demographic group. For party affiliation, the difference between partisans and respondents with no party affiliation is statistically significant, but the differences among Democrats, Republicans, and independents are not.

The magnitude of some of these differences is considerable, and we will examine them later in the book. But for our purposes here, it is essential to recognize that, across sociodemographic and political categories, political ambition is just not very common. Born-again Christians may be far more likely than their nonevangelical counterparts to have considered a candidacy, but 85 percent of them have still not thought about it. Women may be far less likely than men to have thought about a political future, but 87 percent of the men we surveyed still have never done so. And college students may be more than twice as likely as high school students to report interest in running for office, but that still translates into only 15 percent of the college subsample. We can examine any subgroup, and the pattern is generally the same: the next generation of potential leaders has not embraced the prospects of political leadership. In the words of Janie, a college sophomore we interviewed, "I can't imagine why anyone—I don't care about race, or where they live, or whether they're a guy or a girl—would ever want to be in politics."

The Relative (Un)Appeal of a Political Career

Reactions to general questions about interest in running for office are instructive. But a future candidacy can seem abstract and far off for young people. So it is important to juxtapose ambition for a political career with aspirations for other professional paths that might seem equally distant in the future.

We can begin by examining responses to two questions we asked in our national survey. First, we presented young people with four career options—business owner, teacher, mayor of a city or town, and salesperson—and asked which they would most and least like to be, assuming that each job paid the same amount of money. The top half of Figure 2.2 presents the first-choice rankings. Mayor of a town placed a distant third, behind a career in business or teaching. It was a more popular last choice, nearly tying with salesperson for the least desirable of the four professions (see bottom of Figure 2.2).

We then asked the high school and college students to consider a second scenario and tell us which of the following four higher echelon jobs they found most appealing: business executive, lawyer, school principal, or member of Congress. Once again, preferences for careers in the fields of business and education dwarfed interest in a political career. Member of Congress was the least popular option (see top half of Figure 2.3). Indeed, nearly three times as many young people chose a career in business (37 percent), as opposed to a career in politics (13 percent), as their preference. School principal appealed to twice as many as did serving in the US House of Representatives or Senate. On the other hand, young people were significantly more likely to eschew a congressional career than any of the three alternatives. Nearly four out of ten ranked it dead last, making it the least desirable profession (see bottom of Figure 2.3).

These scenarios suggest pretty convincingly that today's young people are not interested in running for office. But what if some of the high school and college students found all of the options unappealing? Or, what if they found several of them attractive and had to choose? In either case, the results might not fully reflect young people's interest in holding public office. Thus, in another attempt to measure political ambition, we provided a list of 20 jobs and asked the survey respondents to check off any they would be open to in the future.

Figure 2.2 Young People's Attitudes toward Being a Mayor

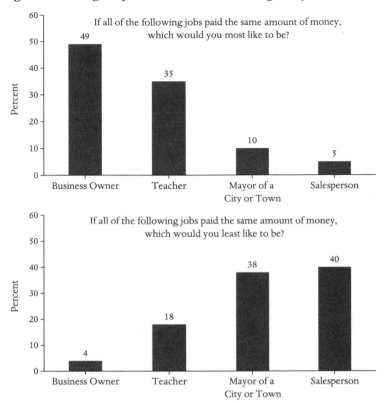

Notes: N = 4,239. Bars indicate the percentage of respondents who chose each career as most (top panel) and least (bottom panel) preferable, when compared to the other three.

Figure 2.3 Young People's Attitudes toward Being a Member of Congress

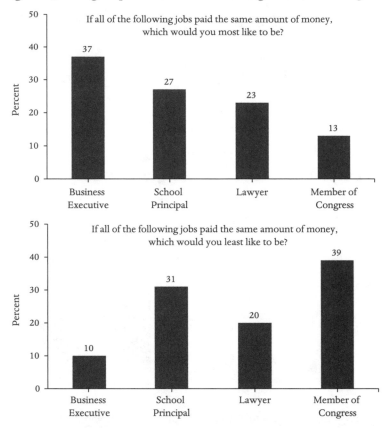

Notes: N = 4,198. Bars indicate the percentage of respondents who chose each career as most (top panel) and least (bottom panel) preferable, when compared to the other three.

The left-hand column of Table 2.2 presents the percentage of young people who were willing to consider each of the jobs we presented to them. As was the case in the career scenarios questions, business and education topped the list. Nearly 30 percent of high school and college students expressed interest in a career in business, and more than one-quarter indicated an interest in teaching. Beyond those fields, they reported interest in a wide range of potential professional pursuits, from medicine to law to journalism to law enforcement. Serving in public office, however, was not among them. Mayor of a city or town was the most appealing political position, but it placed only 12th on the list of 20. Fewer than 10 percent of respondents were interested in the job. An even smaller proportion was open to serving as a member of Congress or as president.

Table 2.2 Jobs Young People Are Willing to Consider for the Future

Full Sample		Those Interested in Three Jobs or Fewer	
Business owner	28.2%	Business owner	16.3%
Teacher	26.1	Teacher	16.3
Artist	21.2	Artist	13.8
Scientist	18.1	Doctor	11.9
Doctor	17.1	Scientist	11.7
Charity work	16.4	Nurse	9.5
Lawyer	14.7	Charity work	7.8
Nurse	13.2	Military	6.0
Journalist	12.5	Lawyer	5.8
Military	10.7	Journalist	5.4
Police officer	9.9	Police officer	5.3
Mayor of a city or town	**9.3**	Professional athlete	4.9
Salesperson	9.2	Secretary	3.4
Member of Congress	**8.8**	Mechanic	3.4
Professional athlete	8.2	Salesperson	3.1
Secretary	8.0	Construction	2.6
Mechanic	6.6	**Mayor of a city or town**	**1.9**
President	**6.4**	**Member of Congress**	**1.6**
Construction	5.6	**President**	**1.6**
Electrician or plumber	3.1	Electrician or plumber	0.9
N	4,280	N	3,111

Notes: Entries indicate the percentage of respondents willing to consider each job as a future career option. The right-hand column is restricted to respondents who have already narrowed their career options to no more than three. Columns do not add to 100% because respondents could check off multiple jobs.

Although previous research has not examined young people's political ambition broadly, a 2004 national poll did ask teenagers whether they would ever want to be president. Comparing those results with ours suggests a marked decline in ambition for the White House. Whereas only about 6 percent of our survey respondents were open to the possibility of being president, 20 percent of 12–17-year-olds expressed interest in the job just eight years earlier.[10] We now live in a time when more young people aspire to be a mechanic or salesperson than president of the United States.

When we turn to only those young people who have already begun to narrow their career preferences, political careers fare even worse in the mix. Roughly 73 percent of the high school and college students indicated interest in no more than three of the 20 jobs we listed. As we would expect, interest in each job drops considerably. But the top 11 choices look quite similar. When we focus on political positions, however, mayor, member of Congress, and president drop to 17th, 18th, and 19th place, respectively (see right-hand column of Table 2.2). Fewer than 2 percent of respondents who have narrowed their career preferences remain willing to consider each of these elective positions. The only job that garners less interest is electrician or plumber.

Willing to Help, Unwilling to Serve

The final way that a lack of political ambition emerged from our survey results can be seen in young people's priorities for the future. We asked about 11 life goals and the importance of achieving each of them. Notably, more than three-quarters of young people reported that improving their community was an "important" or "very important" goal (see Figure 2.4). This places it only slightly below getting married and on par with having children. Making their communities a better place was a goal for more young people than was world travel, religious devotion, or fame. But the survey results show that improving the community and becoming a political leader are not at all synonymous, or even closely linked, in young people's minds. Becoming a political leader ranked last among young people's life goals. In fact, even two-thirds of the people who said that improving their community was a "very important" life goal did not consider becoming a political leader an "important" or "very important" priority for the future.

Figure 2.4 Young People's Goals for the Future

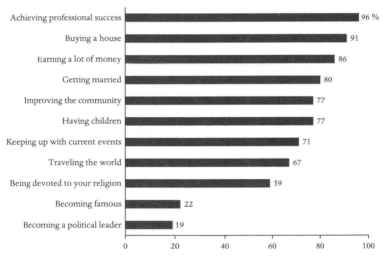

Notes: N = 4,219. Bars indicate the percentage of respondents who consider each goal "important" or "very important" when thinking about the future.

Young people's willingness to serve, but unwillingness to run, is more striking in light of the substantial proportion of high school and college students who are worried about explicitly political issues. More than seven out of ten were concerned about how the economy will affect their lives, and almost 50 percent were concerned about their parents' economic futures. More than half expressed worry about war and terrorism in the near future. Many were also concerned about other contemporary political issues, such as global warming, immigration, and gun violence. On average, the students we surveyed were "very worried" about more than three of the eight major issues we listed. Only a handful expressed worry over none (see Table 2.3).

Table 2.3 Young People's Concerns about the Future

When you think about the future, are you worried about any of the following issues?	
A bad economy preventing you from getting a job	71%
War	55
A terrorist attack in the United States	52
Parents losing their jobs because of a bad economy	47
Global warming or serious harm to the environment	44
Gun violence	36
Failure to deal with illegal immigration	28
None	3
Mean number of issues "very worried" about	3.5
N	4,280

Notes: Entries indicate the percentage of respondents who report being "very worried" about each issue. Numbers do not total 100 percent because respondents could be very worried about multiple issues.

Yet almost invariably, they did not equate addressing these issues, serving their communities, or improving society with political leadership. To those who identified improving the community as an important life goal, we asked in the interviews whether they thought that running for office could be an effective way to achieve it. Although their preferred methods varied, no one considered electoral politics as the most desirable route to pursue. In fact, many stated explicitly that they did not think running for office was a good choice. Consider the following examples:

There are more effective ways to help the community than running for office. Maybe starting a community group or leveraging your business to make change. It is more likely you can do things that way. (Adam, college sophomore)

There are alternatives to running for office if you want to help the community. Look at Exxon. They're building a program for engineers. Corporate America should step up and try to solve the problems of the nation. They have so much money they could definitely be effective. (Bryce, college junior)

In terms of helping to improve the world, I think it is better to work from outside of politics. When you work from the outside, it is easier to see solutions. When you are on the inside, you get caught up in the politics. (Leo, college senior)

I don't think running for office is a very effective way to deal with political issues. Once you get elected, you have a lot more to deal with than just solving problems. If you want to solve a problem in the country, you would be better off starting your own group. (Matt, college sophomore)

My most important life goal is improving the world. I'm a big environmental activist and I'd like to be able to do something to improve the environment with my job. But if I cared about an issue, politics is not the way to go. A better way is to start spreading the word in your community. (Aliza, high school senior)

I really want to improve the world. I get so frustrated with the way things are, and I'd like to work to make things better. . . . I think maybe the best way to get involved would be with a nonprofit. (Alissa, high school senior)

These views were even common among those explicitly interested in public policy. Amanda, a junior at an Ivy League university, explained that her long-term goal is to "improve the world," but she will likely do it by working as a diplomat or for an embassy: "You get a better perspective when you're not in Congress. When you're a politician, you don't really interact with many people or learn about their problems. You're removed from the people." Fabio, a pre-law student, tapped into a similar theme when he explained, "If you're a creative person, then choosing not to run for office is probably the most effective thing you can do to solve problems in society." Because creative people can "come up with new and interesting ways to do something to solve the problem and get people on board with your idea," he told us, "they shouldn't waste their time in politics." Clearly, the passion for positive change exists. But electoral politics as a mechanism to bring it about? Not so much.

Conclusion

We have known for quite some time that young Americans are less politically interested and engaged than older Americans. Young people are also less enthusiastic about government and the global standing of the United States. A 2011 Pew poll revealed that 27 percent of 18–29 year olds think that the United States is the greatest nation in the world. This compares to 38 percent of those 30–49, 40 percent of those 50–64, and 50 percent of those 65 and older.[11] Until now, though, no one has examined what this might mean for young people's political ambition.

Our survey results and interviews tell a straightforward, consistent story: most young people have no interest in running for office. This is the case regardless of how we ask the question or examine the data. There may be more than half a million elective positions to fill, but the overwhelming majority of high school and college students—most of whom have thought seriously about their future career prospects—are anything but eager to rise to the occasion.

The conclusions we draw in this chapter are remarkable because our survey results likely overstate political ambition. After all, these results are based on questions that required young people at least to consider whether they might be interested in running for office. In our open-ended interview questions, which allowed 115 young people to describe their career interests, only four raised on their own the possibility of becoming an elected leader:

- Jason, a 22-year-old business major who "always wants to fix things," would "like to be the president because he deals with different situations—things like health insurance and unemployment and roads." Jason thinks he could "make good decisions on those issues" because he is "good at budgeting, which is important to the president. The budget is really big right now."
- Juan, the grandson and nephew of law-enforcement officials, plans to become a police officer when he graduates from college, but, eventually, he hopes to run for mayor: "It's on my bucket list. . . . I want to do something good for my neighborhood. And the power really appeals to me, too."
- Stephanie, a self-described control-freak who plans to major in marketing or advertising when she gets to college, considers herself a leader, so she thinks "it would be cool to lead a town, or a city, or even the country."
- Tom, a college sophomore at a small school in the Midwest, believes that politics allows you to "engage people in ways no one else can; it's unique in that people trust you with their lives." He plans to enter a city council race so that he can "see how it is to run a campaign." Tom then hopes to

"move on to the state legislature and see where it goes." (He stipulated, though, that he would want to be "pretty far along" in his career before considering a federal race.)

And notice that only Tom identified any sort of path for achieving his political goals.

It is not our position that every young person should demonstrate a willingness to run for office or dream of being a political leader. But when almost 90 percent of young people have either never thought about it, or have ruled it out as dreadful, we can't help but worry about the health of US democracy. The remainder of this book highlights the many ways that perceptions of a broken, dysfunctional government stunt young people's political ambition, and suggests what we can do about it.

3

Not Under My Roof: Politics
in Contemporary American Families

Alex, a conservative teenager from Ohio, loves Ronald Reagan
and sings the praises of supply-side economics. He reads the *Wall
Street Journal* every morning and stares adoringly at the Richard
Nixon headshot on his bedside table every night. When he's not
at a meeting of the Young Republicans Club, he's ridiculing his
former-hippie parents about their concerns over nuclear weapons, environmental degradation, and the precarious future of
PBS. When Alex graduates from college, he knows it will only
be a matter of time before he runs for office. He can't envision a
career more honorable than being a politician.

That was Alex P. Keaton, the character played by Michael
J. Fox on the long-running 1980s sitcom *Family Ties*. Rumored
to be President Reagan's favorite television show, the series was
somewhat unusual in how explicitly politics served as a backdrop
in the Keaton family's daily lives.[1] By devoting full episodes to
the Equal Rights Amendment, US-Soviet relations, and sexual ha-
rassment, the show regularly incorporated politics into conversations that mostly took place at the kitchen table. But the fact that
the family viewed politics as a topic for debate and deliberation,

and politicians—even those on the opposite side of the political aisle—as members of a noble profession was not atypical on television at that time.[2]

From the 1960s through the early 1990s, it was fairly common to flip through the channels and see families—on shows that were not about politics—talking about the political issues of the day. In some cases, characters on television in the mid- to late 20th century even had earnest political aspirations. Consider the 1960 *Leave It to Beaver* episode in which Wally Cleaver, the oldest son in the family, was less than enthused about receiving a nomination for sophomore class president. His father, Ward, questioned his reluctance: "Seems to me it's something to be proud of." He convinced his son to throw himself into the campaign and do everything he could to win.[3] *The Brady Bunch, Diff'rent Strokes, Growing Pains,* and *The Wonder Years* are among many shows that portrayed young people talking about politics with their families, campaigning for candidates, or running for student government. Participating in the democratic process was a good thing to do.

By the mid-1990s, though, characters like Alex P. Keaton had gone the way of the rotary dial phone. As the political climate became increasingly partisan and polarized, politics—even embodied in races for student council—rarely made its way into family sitcoms. *Modern Family*, which became popular soon after it first aired in 2009, exemplifies this change. According to series creators Steve Levitan and Christopher Lloyd, the show focuses less on "how families interact with the outside world; more . . . on how they function internally." As a result, "The roiling topics of politics and religion" are not addressed, but "the simmering topics of sexuality, technology, and dysfunction are."[4]

In the rare instances when politics surfaces in the plotlines of today's sitcoms, it is often to mock or belittle politicians. Again, we can look to *Modern Family*. When Claire Dunphy, one of the show's main characters, runs for the city council because she wants to put a stop sign at a busy intersection, her campaign is portrayed as a substance-free mockery. Questions quickly arise as to why she would ever want to be in politics. And her family cannot even pull itself together to help her get out the vote on Election Day.[5]

Pop culture may be just one indicator of what is important to the average family. But as the presence of politically active families on television has waned, the value placed on discussing politics in actual American families seems to have eroded as well.[6] This absence of politics in contemporary families serves as the first of our three explanations for low political ambition among young people. Our survey results and interviews paint a family portrait in which politics is rarely a household priority. Young people do not frequently talk about politics at home, and seldom do they participate in any political activities with their parents. Few report that their parents have ever suggested that they run for office when they're older, and most get the sense that their parents would prefer them to do something else. Especially important for our purposes, we find that part of the reason families do not discuss politics is because they see it as off-putting, negative, and frustrating. When political engagement in families does occur, it plants the seeds for political ambition. The current political environment, however, makes it quite uncommon for young people to develop this foundation.

All in the Family: Young People's Introduction to Politics

Exposure to politics begins in the family. More than half a century of research compellingly shows that family is the most important influence shaping how young people arrive at their political beliefs.[7] Of course, people can develop an interest in politics later in life, party affiliation can change and evolve over time, and specific circumstances and events can motivate adults to become politically engaged.[8] But the basis for most political attitudes and behaviors comes from what is learned in the family from a young age.

When young people register to vote, for example, their initial party affiliation is often determined by whether their parents identify as Republicans, Democrats, or independents. More generally, adults' ideas about good citizenship, political activism, and political interest can be traced back to the childhood home. Politically engaged parents tend to create family environments that emphasize and value civic engagement. And these messages affect adolescents' behavior. Teenagers who discuss politics with their parents know more about public affairs and are more likely to vote, attend community meetings, sign petitions, participate in boycotts, and contribute money to candidates and political causes.[9]

Women and men who are politically interested and ambitious also often recount childhood memories that were steeped in politics. Throughout the last 15 years, we have surveyed and interviewed thousands of women and men who work in the professions that most often precede political candidacies. Time and again, these potential candidates—most are in their late 40s and early 50s—refer to their early family experiences as setting the stage for their political interest later in life. Jim Heller, for example, is a teacher from Texas and has been politically active since high school. He remembered that "seven out of every ten conversations at the dinner table were about politics. That really left an imprint." When we asked Jill Steinberg, a lawyer from Florida, about her initial interest in politics, she also referred to her childhood: "I remember as a kid that I talked to my parents about becoming the first female Supreme Court judge. When Sandra Day O'Connor got the appointment, I remember thinking, darn, I wanted that." Tony Arriaga, a litigator from Chicago, told us that politics in his family is "in the genes." He recalled, "My parents took me with them on Election Day from the time I could walk. They took me to political meetings and fundraisers from as far back as I can remember. And they always told me that their parents did the same." These early political experiences and impressions definitely left a mark. When he was in his mid-30s, Arriaga ran for a local office in his community. A few years later, he sought a seat at the county level.[10]

A Portrait of the Contemporary (and Apolitical) Family

If we want to understand the roots of why young people are turned off to politics, an important starting point is clearly the family. We begin by examining the various ways that politics and current events surface in young people's homes. Or, as the survey results make clear, how little they do. The vast majority of today's high school and college students live with (or grew up in) families that do not prioritize following the news or keeping up with current events. Three-quarters of the students we surveyed said that their parents do not regularly talk about politics; only one in five identified it as a regular topic of conversation at mealtime. An even smaller proportion described living in a household where lively political discussion ever occurs (see top of Table 3.1).[11]

The results are similar when we focus on specific topics of political conversation between young people and their parents. We included on the survey questions about whether our respondents had ever—even just once—talked to their parents about three major policy issues: the wars in Iraq and Afghanistan, marriage equality, and climate change. In each case, and during the heat of the 2012 presidential election, when these issues received a fair amount of media attention, roughly 60 percent reported never discussing these topics with their parents.

Table 3.1 Political Engagement in Young People's Families

Politics in the Household	
Parents often talk about politics with friends and family.	25 %
Family often talks about politics at mealtime.	21
Parents sometimes yell at the TV because they are mad about politics.	16
Political Discussion with Parents	
Speaks with mother about politics at least a few times a week.	21
Speaks with father about politics at least a few times a week.	23
Speaks with mother about politics rarely or never.	51
Speaks with father about politics rarely or never.	49
Political Activity with Parents	
Went to vote with parents.	26
Attended a political event with parents.	6
Watched election coverage with parents.	37
Shared a story on email or a social networking site with parents.	20
N	4,280

Notes: Entries indicate the percentage of respondents who answered each question affirmatively or engaged in each activity. Responses from college students who no longer live at home reflect patterns of political engagement when they did live with their parents. For the "Political Discussion with Parents" questions, the sample size is 3,853 for questions pertaining to a mother and 3,188 for questions pertaining to a father. The missing cases result from family units that do not include two parents.

Approximately half said they rarely or never discussed politics whatsoever with either their mothers or their fathers (see middle of Table 3.1). Keep in mind, too, that these results likely reflect a best-case scenario. After all, if political discussion was ever going to take place at home, the hotly contested 2012 presidential election would have been a likely time for it to happen.

Given the little political discussion in most homes, it is not surprising that it is also unusual for young people to do anything political with their parents, such as go with them to vote or watch even a little bit of election coverage. And it's not only traditional political acts that rarely occur. Despite the extent to which Facebook, Twitter, and other social media have become key tools for communication, four out of five high school and college students have never emailed or shared a political story or current event with their parents (see bottom of Table 3.1).

Now, it is important to recognize that the patterns we just described paint the average family with broad strokes. Of course, not all families are the same. But tree-hugging liberals who always vote for the Democrats and gun-carrying Tea Partiers who consistently support the Republicans actually do have something in common: politics is far more likely to make it into their family discussions than those with less partisan parents. More specifically, 39 percent of high school and college students with two parents who affiliate with one of the major political parties talked regularly with them about politics. The number drops to 26 percent for high school and college students with just one partisan parent. And it dips to just 11 percent in homes with no parent registered as either a Democrat or Republican. Young people with at least one partisan parent were also more than two and a half times as likely as those without (26 percent compared to 10 percent) to talk about politics at mealtimes. The gaps are even larger when we compare the 25 percent of young people who identified at least one of their parents as a "strong Democrat" or "strong Republican" to those who did not.

In general, though, families are not talking politics. Our interviews reinforced this finding; 84 of the 115 people we interviewed said their parents did not actively encourage them to be politically aware; more than half (62) could not recall *any* specific political discussion or conversation with their parents. But this wasn't always the case. In the 1970s, high school seniors were 50 percent more likely than they are today to talk regularly to their parents about politics.[12] Indeed, scholars, pundits, and activists have lamented this shift for some time. A 2005 Brookings Institution report about the health of American democracy opens by characterizing it as "at risk." The authors argue that the risk "comes not from some external threat but from disturbing internal trends: an erosion of the activities and capacities of citizenship. Americans have turned away from politics and the public sphere in large numbers, leaving our civic life impoverished."[13]

The Dinner Table Is No Place for Politics

By analyzing the content of the interviews, we can begin to understand why politics so infrequently surfaces in young people's homes. The following excerpt from the transcript of our conversation with Andrew, a 20-year-old engineering student from New York, resembles many from the interviews we conducted:

Question: Would you say that your parents are interested in politics?

Andrew: *No, not really. I think that more recently they have begun to realize that some social programs are very important. But that's about it.*

Question: Do they ever talk about politics around the house or at meals?

Andrew: *No. We weren't very political growing up.*

Question: Did your parents encourage you to follow politics, or be interested in current events and what was going on in the world?

Andrew: *No, not really.*

Question: Did they, or do they, tell you it's important to vote?

Andrew: *Yeah. That we knew. They didn't directly say it, but I remember going with them to vote.*

Question: Why do you think politics and current events were not more important in your family when you were growing up?

Andrew: *I think it was because we were all busy and it all seemed too negative. We didn't actually spend that much time talking together about anything. So, when we did have a chance, it would not have been much fun to talk about politics.*

Tatiana, a college sophomore from California, recounted a similar dynamic in her home:

Question: Would you say that your parents are interested in politics?

Tatiana: *Oh, I don't know. I'd really have to ask them.*

Question: Do they ever talk about politics around the house or at meals?

Tatiana: *No. That never happens.*

Question: Did your parents encourage you to follow politics, or be interested in current events and what was going on in the world?

Tatiana: *Not really.*

Question: Did they, or do they, tell you it's important to vote?

Tatiana: *Well, I remember going with them to vote a couple of times. So, in that way, they made it seem important.*

Question: Why do you think politics and current events were not more important in your family when you were growing up?

Tatiana: *What would we have talked about? A bunch of guys fighting with each other and not getting anything done?*

As these excerpts indicate, two themes emerged in our conversations: keeping up with politics and current affairs is just not an important part of family life; and politics is perceived as so negative and contentious that it is an unappealing topic of conversation.

Doug, a high school senior from Arizona, lives in a household that epitomizes these circumstances. When we asked whether his parents have impressed upon him the importance of politics, Doug said, "They don't really encourage me. They do tell me to be aware of what's going on . . . but we just don't talk about political stuff that much." Or consider Hadleigh, a college senior who will graduate with a degree in elementary education. She characterized her parents as "not very interested in current events," although they "usually vote and know who they want to win an election. But that is about it." She recalled little political conversation in the household: "At the dinner table, we just never spoke about politics. I have younger siblings and they were too little to discuss these things."

When we pressed students like Doug and Hadleigh and asked if they think it is important to care about current events and the world around them, the second theme emerged. The young people we interviewed almost always offered what has become a socially desirable response: it is important to stay informed about politics. But they quickly cited the hostile and dysfunctional political climate as a deterrent. Doug acknowledged, for example, that he would "probably be more into [politics] if [his] parents cared more. But growing up, it was obvious that they hated all the bickering in politics, so that just rubbed off." Hadleigh concurred: "Politics is very important, and I wish I had been more encouraged to follow it. But I think my parents thought it was all so complicated and such a mess that there was no point."

Doug and Hadleigh's reflections were echoed by many of the others we interviewed. Mindy, a college junior, shared her earliest political memory, which also turned out to be the last time she remembers speaking with her mother about politics:

I remember when I was little and the scandal with Bill Clinton and Monica Lewinsky was on TV. My mom did not want to tell me what it was about and turned off the television. She said all the politicians were bad. That is the last time I remember discussing politics with my mom, and I was, like, six.

The lack of political discussion in David's household is not linked to a specific politician, but, rather, a general distaste toward them all. The high school senior explained, "In my family, we just don't talk about political stuff that much . . . I get the sense from my parents that Washington and politicians are terrible and a million miles away. That we just should not bother with it." Jane's parents told her to vote, but they never talked about politics at home: "The fact that they never really wanted to talk about government stuff conveyed to me that it's just not very important. And when it did come up, they were always saying that the system was too broken to pay attention to."

Of course, politics is not off limits in all households. Roughly one-quarter of the young people we surveyed live in or grew up in homes with regular political discussion and debate (see Table 3.1). But even in these families, conversations often center on the troubling nature of contemporary times. Lizbeth, a geography major at a large university, remarked, "My parents always urged us to get involved and make the world a better place. . . . We have big debates at dinner about important issues. But we often end up condemning the whole government system for being so ridiculous." Evan, a high school sophomore, described the nightly ritual of sitting down to dinner and listening to his parents "critique the government. They speak on and on about how corrupt politicians are."

Some young people offered more colorful examples of political discussion in their homes. Consistent with the partisan times in which we live, Megan, a business major, recalled regular condemnation of President Bush: "My parents were always talking about how stupid Bush was. It was kind of funny, but it sort of made me think the president was a joke." Others were regularly exposed to conversations about how much their parents detest President Obama. Fabio, a college pre-law major, described his household this way: "My Dad is always watching the news and telling us how Obama is going to destroy America. He can get so mad. He will be muttering around the house about how Obama is ruining this or shredding the Constitution." Sean, a high school sophomore, always hears his father "talking about how bad the Democrats are, and how they want to tax us to death. He tells us that only the Republicans are sane."

Whether we focus on the national survey results or the interviews, the story is the same: politics is rarely a topic of family discussion. Most parents convey to their children that voting is important, but that is where messages of civic engagement seem to end. Very few parents urge their children to stay informed politically or to keep abreast of current events. Parents with busy lives, many of whom are struggling to get by likely see little point in discussing with their families the latest failure in Washington, DC, or the most recent negative campaign ad on the television screen. Although political disengagement—both by adults and young people—is not a new phenomenon, recent polls and surveys suggest that it is worse now than in previous generations. And our analysis makes clear that the current tenor of US politics is one of the causes.

Hey Kid, You Really Shouldn't Run for President Someday

Frequent family conversations about politics are certainly important indicators of young people's exposure to it. But parents and family members who directly encourage young people to run for office send an even stronger message about the value of political engagement. So, we asked the high school and college students whether any members of their family ever suggested that they become leaders in their communities and run for office someday. Parents are more likely than grandparents, aunts and uncles, and siblings to suggest to their sons and daughters a future as an elected official. But overall, young people receive little encouragement to consider entering politics later in life (see Table 3.2). Three-quarters of parents have never encouraged their children to consider it, even in passing. Just slightly more than 5 percent of the young people we surveyed reported that either their mother or father routinely encouraged them to run for office.

Table 3.2 Family Encouragement for Young People to Run for Office

Have any of the following people ever suggested that someday you should become a leader in your community and run for office?	
Parent	26 %
Grandparent	11
Aunt or uncle	7
Brother or sister	7
Frequency of Parental Encouragement to Run for Office	
Mother has never mentioned it.	72
Father has never mentioned it.	74
Mother has suggested it a number of times.	5
Father has suggested it a number of times.	6
N	4,280

Notes: Entries in the top half of the table indicate the percentage of respondents who report that each family member suggested a future candidacy. In the bottom half of the table, the sample size is 3,855 for questions pertaining to a mother and 3,183 for questions pertaining to a father. The missing cases result from family units that do not include two parents.

Less than 2 percent said that they received regular encouragement from both parents.[14]

Beyond not receiving encouragement from their parents to run for office, young people also perceive that their parents would prefer that they do something else with their lives. We included on the survey a question that listed five jobs, and we asked students to identify which one they thought their parents would most like to see them pursue. Figure 3.1 summarizes the results. Approximately half thought that their mothers and fathers would prefer them to own a business. Roughly 30 percent perceived that their parents would most like them to pursue a career in education, either as a teacher or professor. When we turn to the remaining 20 percent, perceived preferences split among professional athlete, member of Congress, and member of the clergy. Overall, this means that of five possible career paths, less than one out of every ten young people ranked member of Congress as their parents' likely preference for them.

Figure 3.1 Young People's Perceptions of their Parents' Job Preferences for Them

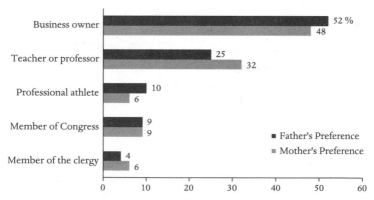

Notes: N = 3,807 for respondents' perceptions of the job they think their mother would most like them to pursue, and N = 3,146 for respondents' perceptions of the job they think their father would most like them to pursue.

Once again, partisanship plays an important role in the careers that parents want their children to pursue. The national Republican Party adopts and touts far more antigovernment rhetoric than the Democratic Party does. Our data suggest that Republican parents repeat many of these positions at home, conveying to their children that being a politician is not a very exciting or respectable career choice. In Republican homes, children are most likely to say that their parents would want them to work in business. Children of Democratic parents, on the other hand, are more likely to think that their parents would like to see them pursue a career in law, education, or government. More specifically, children with "strong Democratic" mothers are nearly twice as likely as those with "strong Republican" mothers to report that their mothers would prefer them to be in Congress, as opposed to the other four professions. The party difference is similar for fathers.

It is not only strong partisanship that matters; parents who merely affiliate with one of the two major parties are perceived as more likely than those who do not to want their children to run for office. More specifically, only 5 percent of young people without at least one parent who identifies as a Democrat or Republican think that their parent(s) would like to see them serve in the US Congress. That portion increases to 12 percent for people with one parent who affiliates with one of the two major parties, and to 17 percent for those with two parents who affiliate with a party. Still, most young people, regardless of their parents' party affiliation or strength of partisanship, do not believe that their mothers or fathers would like to see them run for office later in life.[15]

We found the same general pattern in the interviews: young people did not get the sense that their parents would be particularly happy or enthusiastic on learning that their children wanted to go into politics and eventually run for Congress. Gavin, a high school senior, was particularly blunt: "My parents just wouldn't want that for me. They would want me to do something that would make me happy." Becca, a high school sophomore, voiced concern that her father might be disappointed. "He knows a lot about people in Congress and he doesn't like them," she explained. "I don't think he'd be pleased because he didn't raise me to be like them." Others insinuated that their parents would think that going into politics would not allow their sons and daughters to achieve their full potential. James, a college sophomore who has not yet declared a major, told us that his parents would likely be "somewhat neutral" if he told them he wanted to run for office at some point in the future. But, because "they have a negative view on a lot of things about government, including politicians," he thinks they would prefer he spend his time "doing something important." Sydney, a high school senior, shared a similar impression: "My Mom would probably be fine with it. But I am sure that if she could choose, she'd want me to do something else. She knows I can do more than that."

Unlike Gavin, Becca, James, and Sydney, the majority explained that their parents would "be supportive of anything [they] want to do," and that "as long as [they're] happy, it doesn't matter." But many also expected that their parents would be concerned if they chose politics. Matthew, a high school junior who described his relationship with his parents as one in which they "encourage [him] any way they can," acknowledged that "they might be a little worried about getting involved with politics." Hayden's parents "would probably be okay with it," but the 11th grader went on to speculate that "they would probably want [her] to do something else." A college senior, Simone told us that she and her parents have recently had several conversations about what she wants to do when she graduates. Although politics has never been in the mix, she thinks her parents would likely be supportive, although not enthusiastic: "I don't think they'd hate me for it, but I don't think they'd be as happy as if I said I was doing something else. Whenever we've talked about politics, it seems to me that they don't think people in Congress have that much of an effect."

In several cases, our conversations revealed that young people do not think that their parents would want them to enter the political fray because of the spectacle involved in contemporary campaigns and elections. As Samantha, a college junior, reflected, "They'd be very hesitant about me getting into the spotlight like that." TJ, a high school senior, concluded that his parents would probably be leery about "how everyone would look into everything [they've] ever done." Concerns about a lack of privacy and skeletons in the closet emerged in multiple interviews:

> They would be proud of me, but they wouldn't want me to run. It'd put their lives in jeopardy since their privacy would be destroyed. (Geoffrey, high school freshman)

> They would want to be supportive, but they couldn't. I know they'd say it's too late for me, that I have already done too many crazy things that the public would learn about. (Jack, college sophomore)

> My mom and dad would be supportive, but skeptical. They would worry about whether I could handle the pressure of a campaign. And about whether I could take the constant attacks. (Vivian, college junior)

Even those who relayed to us that their parents would likely be happy if they ultimately decided to run for office conveyed a sense that they would still be taken aback by the announcement. Anna, for example, is an 11th grader who hopes to major in political science when she goes to college. Although she and her parents often discuss politics and current events, she thinks that they would "be in shock" if she ever told them she actually wanted to run for office herself: "They'd be happy I guess. They definitely wouldn't be mad or anything like that. But after all the conversations we've had about what's wrong with Washington, I don't think they'd believe that I'd ever really be happy doing that." Johanna, a college sophomore, responded similarly: "They might tell me to go for it if it would make me happy. But they probably wouldn't show much interest. Probably because they couldn't possibly imagine that it would ever make me happy."

We must be somewhat cautious when interpreting these impressions. Young people have a sense of what their parents would like them to do later in life, but, without speaking to the parents, we should be careful when drawing broad conclusions. The perceptions of our survey respondents, however, are consistent with national polling data from adults. In December 2013, Gallup asked a national random sample of Americans to rate the honesty and ethics of people who work in 22 different professions. Whereas more than 80 percent of people think that nurses have "high" or "very high" honesty and ethics, and roughly 70 percent have faith in pharmacists, teachers, doctors, and military officers, politicians fare significantly worse. Less than 25 percent of Americans rate local officeholders—such as mayors, city councilors, and school board members—as high or very high on ethics. The number is nearly cut in half for state officeholders (14 percent). Members of Congress are considered honest and ethical by less than 10 percent of the population. Only lobbyists perform worse, and not by much (see Table 3.3).

These negative evaluations are even more damning when placed in historical context. In the 1970s, 1980s, and early 1990s, Americans were two to three times more likely than they are today to rate members of Congress "high" or "very high" on honesty and ethics. At the other end of the continuum, the percentage of people who scored members of Congress "very low" on ethics and honesty hovered at around 10 percent. In the 2013 Gallup poll, that number had climbed to a record 30 percent.[16] Politics is just not viewed as a worthwhile, important endeavor. Most people think that the system is dysfunctional and that its players lack honesty and ethics. They'd rather their children do almost anything else.

Table 3.3 Public Attitudes about the Honesty and Ethics of People in Various Professions

	"High" or "Very High" on Honesty and Ethics
Nurses	82 %
Pharmacists	70
Grade-school teachers	70
Medical doctors	69
Military officers	69
Police officers	54
Clergy	47
Day-care providers	46
Judges	45
Nursing home operators	32
Auto mechanics	29
Bankers	27
Local officeholders	**23**
Business executives	22
Newspaper reporters	21
Lawyers	20
Television reporters	20
Advertising practitioners	14
State officeholders	**14**
Car salespeople	9
Members of Congress	**8**
Lobbyists	6

Notes: Data are from a national Gallup poll (December 5–8, 2013).

The Consequences of a Politically Alienated Family

Family members, particularly parents, play a critical role in shaping young people's lives and goals. In fact, when we asked the high school and college students about their sources of inspiration when thinking about the future, more than two-thirds identified their mother, and more than half identified their father.[17] Parents' active roles in their children's lives were also evident in responses to questions about how family decisions are made and how young people decide what activities to pursue. Modern households tend to be collaborative, with four out of five young people reporting that their parents value and take into consideration their children's opinions when making decisions. Similarly, 80 percent said that their parents have considerable influence over their extracurricular activities and interests. Parents are, quite simply, central to their children's aspirations.

Most parents' distaste for government limits political discussion within the typical household and young people's political exposure. This has a strong and direct influence on interest in running for office. Figure 3.2 highlights the relationship between young people's political ambition and several political experiences in the family. The first set of bars, for example, shows that 22 percent of those who talk about politics with a parent at least a few times a week have considered running for office. Only 6 percent of people who do not talk about politics with a parent at least a few times a week have thought about running. Encouragement from a parent to run for office is even a stronger influence: young people whose parent(s) suggested that they think about a political career were roughly five times as likely as young people who never received such encouragement to be interested in running for office in the future. Encouragement from other relatives also had a substantial effect. These results are consistent with our studies of potential candidates. Those who reported growing up in a household where their parents frequently suggested that they run for office were 70 percent more likely than those who never received parental encouragement to consider running.

Figure 3.2 Political Families and Young People's Political Ambition

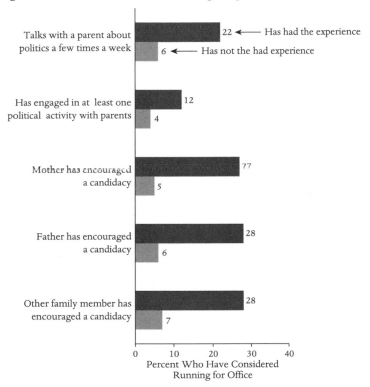

Talks with a parent about politics a few times a week
22 ◄——— Has had the experience
6 ◄——— Has not the had experience

Has engaged in at least one political activity with parents
12
4

Mother has encouraged a candidacy
?7
5

Father has encouraged a candidacy
28
6

Other family member has encouraged a candidacy
28
7

0   10   20   30   40
Percent Who Have Considered
Running for Office

Notes: N = 4,277. Black bars indicate the percentage of respondents who have considered running for office and report having had the family-related experience. Gray bars indicate the percentage of respondents who have considered running for office, but have not had the experience. All differences are statistically significant at p < .05.

Because of the effect that parental encouragement plays in triggering young people's political ambition, the party differences we uncovered earlier manifest themselves here as well.

Approximately 14 percent of young people who grew up with a father or mother who identified as a strong Democrat indicated that they were "definitely interested" in running for office someday, compared to only 5 percent of young people with strong Republican fathers or mothers.

The interviews we conducted confirm the importance of family support in cultivating young people's political aspirations. Although most young people described very apolitical households, some did express at least some interest in or general willingness to consider running for office. And every single one of them mentioned a supportive family.

Anjelica, a 20-year-old biology major, is one such young person. When we asked her if she would like to be president someday, Anjelica responded, "Absolutely." She went on to say that her parents would be "really excited" if she decided to run because they always emphasized the importance of politics:

> I remember going to the polls with my dad. I think we went for the presidential elections and the city elections. I remember a lot of people were there and my dad would tell me a little story about who he was voting for and how where he grew up, his family didn't do things this way. He would talk about how wonderful it was that people had a voice in choosing our leaders.

But Anjelica is not naïve about contemporary politics. She recognizes that "today's politics can be a nasty business," and she noted that her parents "always talk about that part of it, too." On balance, though, she feels that she still "has a lot to offer."

Thomas, a 21-year-old political science major, recounted a similar experience growing up: "I used to always go to vote with my mom. I thought it was cool and patriotic, and that voting was a really cool thing to do." He continued by telling us that although his parents are well aware of the problems in Washington, they still want him to be involved: "My parents really love that I'm into politics. They're really encouraging and always telling me to run for office someday. . . . And I will. Someday, I'd like to be in Congress."

In a final example, Aaron, a high school senior who would like to be an engineer, is also very interested in running for office once his "career gets going." He remembered that both of his parents "volunteered for campaigns and were very interested in politics" when he was younger. They are also very supportive of any way he wants to make a difference in the world. Like Anjelica and Thomas, Aaron is not unfamiliar with the contemporary political scene, noting that he and his parents "are concerned about how negative politics is and how hard it is to get anything done." But he believes that "the only way to make things better is to get involved."

A Note on Girls and Boys: The Gender Gap in Encouragement to Run for Office

Family experiences shape young people's political interest and ambition, but prior research suggests that women are less likely than men to be exposed to politics growing up. Our surveys of lawyers, business leaders, educators, and political activists found that women were nearly 20 percent less likely than men to remember speaking about politics with their fathers; and they were 15 percent less likely than men to report that their parents had encouraged them to run for office. Perhaps as a result of these family experiences, men were two-thirds more likely than women to have first considered running for office before they graduated from high school.[18]

Attitudes about women as leaders have certainly changed over time, and public perceptions of women in politics have evolved. The General Social Survey finds, however, that roughly 25 percent of Americans still believe that men are better suited emotionally for politics than are women. A recent Gallup poll revealed that 14% of citizens still agree that "women aren't tough enough for politics." Sixteen percent of Americans think that "women don't make as good leaders as men."[19] These numbers reflect dramatic improvement from only a few decades ago, but they also indicate that not all citizens view women and men as political equals.

Consistent with these recent polls, we uncovered notable evidence that young women and men, especially by the time they reach college, do not get the same degree of family encouragement to pursue a political candidacy later in life. For the most part, when it comes to having political discussions with parents, going to vote with them, or following news together, young women and men reported nearly identical family experiences. And this was true for both high school and college students. When we turn to encouragement to run for office, though, we see significant gender differences among college students. College men were about 38 percent more likely than college women to report encouragement to run for office from at least one parent (see Figure 3.3). College women were also significantly more likely than college men to think that their parents would prefer them to pursue a career other than politics.

As we demonstrated in the previous section, parents who encourage their children to consider running for office dramatically increase their children's political ambition. Fifty percent of college students whose mothers regularly suggested that they run for office said that they would definitely like to do it in the future. Only 3 percent who received no such encouragement from their mothers expressed interest in a future candidacy. The results are similar for encouragement from fathers; 46 percent whose fathers encouraged a candidacy planned to run for office in the future, compared to 4 percent whose fathers did not.

Figure 3.3 Parental Attitudes toward Sons and Daughters Running for Office

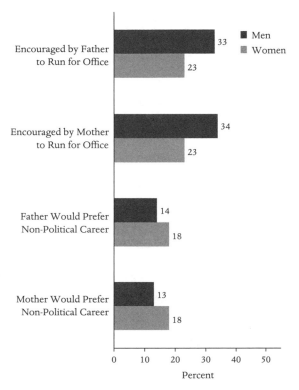

Notes: N = 1,020 for men and 1,097 for women (the analysis includes only the college students in our sample). Bars represent the percentage of men and women who reported parental encouragement to run for office later in life, and that if they told their father or mother that, someday, they wanted to run for office, their parent would prefer that they do something else. All gender differences are statistically significant at p < .05.

We are limited in what we can say about the reason that the gender gap in parental encouragement is so much larger among college than high school students. But the explanation likely lies, at least in part, in the personal and academic freedom that college students enjoy compared to their high school counterparts.

A majority of college students move out of their parents' homes to attend college, and, even when they don't, they often have more independence. Further, whereas high school curricula generally offer little choice, college provides students with a wide array of academic options and electives. Essentially, when students get to college and "the shackles come off," young women and men have much greater control over how they spend their time and what interests they pursue. When this happens, women and men's interests diverge. It may be that parents encourage their sons and daughters to pursue their newfound interests. Because women are less likely than men to express interest in politics, parents may follow their lead and offer less encouragement for them to go down a political path.

Conclusion

During an interview with C-SPAN in January 2014, former First Lady Barbara Bush said that she does not want another son—or any member of her family, for that matter—to run for president of the United States. Fueled by speculation that Jeb Bush, the former Republican governor of Florida, and the brother of President George W. Bush, might throw his hat into the ring in 2016, Mrs. Bush lauded her son's credentials: "There is no question in my mind that Jeb is the best qualified person to run for President." But she quickly went on to say that she hoped he would not. Worried that "he'll get all of [her] enemies, all his brother's," she concluded that "there are lots of ways to serve, and being president is not the only one."[20] (Mrs. Bush's views on her son's presidential aspirations had softened by the time Jeb Bush launched a presidential exploratory committee in December 2014.)

Ann Romney, the wife of former Republican presidential nominee Mitt Romney, sounded a similar chord, telling CNN's Jake

Tapper that she would not embrace another political candidacy in the family:

> I would hesitate—I think it is a very tough thing to do. I think it's a huge sacrifice and I think it is very hurtful many times for the spouse to have to watch the kind of abuse that you know you have to go through. So I'd really have to measure that and think about it and think about the individual circumstance.

When those circumstances involved her son Tagg, who was rumored to be thinking about running for the US Senate seat vacated by John Kerry when he was appointed Secretary of State, Mrs. Romney did not equivocate. "I would say don't do it to Tagg," she said. "I would."[21]

It is easy to justify Barbara Bush and Ann Romney's reluctance. Both experienced grueling times on the campaign trail, a fishbowl level of scrutiny, and defeat on election night. It's no wonder that they would not wish the same for their sons. But they also saw firsthand the upside to electoral politics. Their husbands—one as president and the other as governor—had the capacity to implement sweeping policy change, address the biggest problems facing the country, and shape the political agenda for years to come. The fact that the power and possibilities of elective office do not outweigh the negatives speaks to how the current political system is perceived. Barbara Bush and Ann Romney's circumstances might be uncommon, but their reactions to a political future for their children are typical of—and might even perpetuate—those of an average parent.

The families of today's young people are far less politically connected than the Bushes and Romneys. In fact, as we have demonstrated throughout this chapter, they are not very politically connected at all. Rarely do they discuss politics, and only infrequently do parents encourage their children to think about a political career. When families do talk politics, the discussion is often short and negative. Typical conversations involve mocking politicians, characterizing the system as corrupt, and perpetuating the idea that government is complicated, messy, and ineffective. Because of the extraordinarily unappealing way that the contemporary political environment presents itself to average Americans, who can blame them for shying away from political discussion?

Of course, the results in this chapter also show that when young people are exposed to politics at home, and when their parents do talk to them regularly about the importance of staying aware of what is going on in the world—no matter how negative the conversation may be—they are more ambitious to rise up and become political leaders. As long as the political environment continues to operate as it currently does, though, families will likely continue to be turned off, political exposure and discussion in most homes will remain low, and most young people will never consider running for office.

4

#GovernmentSucks: How Young People Experience Contemporary Politics

In 1997, a former university administrator launched *collegeprep101.com*. The website's mission, as summarized on its home page, is to help students transition to college: "We believe the more you know about what to expect when you get to college, the better prepared you will be to deal with it."[1] Accordingly, the site provides students with a list of items they should bring to college, definitions of "critical" college terms (including words like "faculty" and "syllabus"), and links to financial-aid information. In addition, it features the equivalent of a daily planner of four full-time college students. They all report, by the hour, how they spend a typical week. The students, who attend different schools and major in different fields, have a lot in common. They spend the bulk of their time taking classes, hanging out with their friends, working part-time jobs, and participating in extracurricular activities. They also share what appears to be absolutely no interest in staying abreast of what's going on in the world. None ever mentions following the news or having any sort of political conversation or discussion.[2]

A prospective student who visits the website might conclude that keeping up with current events is not something most college students worry about. And she'd be right. The *American Time Use Survey* more systematically accounts for how college students spend their time. On average, they spend nearly four hours a day playing sports or engaging in leisure activities, which is more than the 3.4 hours they devote to attending classes and studying, or the 2.7 hours they spend at work. College students round out their days with sleep (8.6 hours), travel to and from work and school (1.5 hours), food and drink (one hour), and personal grooming (45 minutes).[3] And texting, of course; the average college-aged adult sends about 90 texts a day.[4] Missing from this list are reading the newspaper, watching the news, or following politics. In fact, an annual study of college freshmen finds that only about one-third believe that keeping up with current events is even an important goal. This percentage is down from the roughly two-thirds of young people who felt this way in the 1960s.[5]

The story is much the same for high school students. Obviously, their time is a little more constrained by the uniformity of school schedules; the average high school student spends more than six hours a day at school. After school, they pass time by watching television (2.1 hours), socializing with friends (one hour), playing video games (45 minutes), and participating in sports (30 minutes).[6] Throughout the day, they also manage to send about 80 text messages.[7] More than half of today's high school students report doing no homework on an average day. And few devote any time whatsoever to following news, current events, or politics.

The high school and college students we surveyed and interviewed for this book reported similar patterns. They dedicate energy to school and extracurricular activities, participate in sports, and spend time with their friends. Most are also glued to their digital devices. About 50 percent play video games every day, more than half spend at least a few hours sending texts and communicating via social media with their friends, and one-third watch at least two hours of television. In each of these realms, exposure to politics is infrequent and not prioritized (much like the family experiences described in chapter 3).

These patterns serve as the basis for our second explanation for low political ambition among young people: limited exposure to politics in their day-to-day lives. We begin this chapter by confirming what others have found to be true about today's high school and college students. Put simply, they do not lead politically connected lives. From their interactions in the classroom and with their teachers, to their relationships with their friends, to the media they consume, politics rarely surfaces. But we go beyond documenting young people's general political disengagement. The second part of the chapter demonstrates how the dysfunction and negativity that have come to characterize the current political environment lead many young people to avoid thinking about it, talking about it, or caring about it. Those who are politically engaged at school, or talk to their friends about current events, or access political information through the media are more politically ambitious than those who don't. But they are few and far between, in large part because contemporary politics has turned them off.

Far from 24/7: Young People's Daily Exposure to Politics

School experiences, friend and peer interactions, and media habits—like family—shape young people's political interest and attitudes. Classroom programs in high schools that include political activities or assignments, for instance, can increase students' intentions to vote and elevate their sense of political empowerment.[8] In college, when students major in social sciences that emphasize the development of civic skills, they are more likely to participate politically.[9] Outside the classroom, young people's participation in extracurricular activities can also spur political interest and civic engagement later in life.[10] Politically active adults are more likely than people who are not politically engaged to recount early involvement in political associations, campaigns, and community service projects. They are also more likely to have run for office in either a high school or college student body election. These activities are important not only because of their politically charged content, but also because conversations within social networks of peers and friends can influence people's attitudes toward, and participation in, politics.[11] And media—particularly internet and digital technologies—can reinforce the civic skills learned inside and outside the classroom, ultimately increasing young people's political interest and voter turnout.[12]

School experiences, relationships with friends and peers, and nearly unfettered access to a wide range of media offer many opportunities for young people to connect to news, politics, and current events. But how often is this potential realized? In order to shed light on that question, the following pages chronicle the daily lives of the young people we surveyed. We frame our analysis through the ordinary weekday schedule of Heidi, a 17-year-old high school honors student who plans to major in psychology when she heads to college. Although we found some differences in how young people lived—when they woke up, which classes they took, what extracurricular activities they pursued, how much time they spent with friends—Heidi's schedule represents that of the typical high school student we interviewed.[13]

7:12 AM—Wake Up, Check Facebook, Text Three Friends
7:55 AM—Head to School (Update Facebook Status along the Way)
8:15 AM—First Class of the Day (English Lit)

Given that political experiences at school exert a significant impact on young people's political engagement, it is vital to examine how much political exposure they receive in their classrooms and on their campuses. Some of this exposure is required by law. Thirty-nine states mandate that high school students take a government or civics class to graduate.[14] The requirement is not as widespread in college, but many states, including California and Texas, require students enrolled in public colleges and universities to complete at least one government class that covers both national and state politics.

Among the high school students we surveyed, only about one-quarter had taken a government class. Most of the students had not yet reached 11th or 12th grade, when such courses are typically offered, so this finding is not surprising. But they also reported very little political content in their other classes. Nearly two-thirds said that they discuss politics in their classes less than once a week, and one-third said that political discussions in the classroom occurred "rarely" or "never." Just 9 percent of high school students considered their classmates "very interested" in politics and current events (see left-hand column of Table 4.1).

College students reported significantly more political exposure in the classroom. Nearly seven out of ten had taken at least one government or political science class, and they were substantially more likely than high school students to have attended a school event where a politician spoke, or to have completed an assignment that required contacting some sort of political leader. They were also twice as likely as the high school students to consider their classmates politically interested (see right-hand column of Table 4.1). Even among the college students, though, weekly political discussions in the classroom were not the norm (32 percent reported having them), and only two out of ten described their classmates as very interested in politics and current events.

Table 4.1 Young People's Political Engagement at School

	High School Students	College Students
Political Exposure at School		
Took a government or political science class	27% *	69%
Attended an assembly or class with a politician as a guest speaker	19 *	29
Contacted a political leader as part of a class assignment	9 *	15
Political Discussion in Classes at School		
Never	6	8
Rarely	25	26
A few times a month	33	33
At least once a week	36	32
Classmates' Interest in Politics		
Not interested	19 *	9
A little interested	46 *	26
Interested	27 *	44
Very interested	9 *	21
N	2,163	2,117

Notes: Sample sizes vary slightly across questions because some respondents omitted answers to some questions. Levels of significance: * indicates that the difference between high school and college students is statistically significant at $p < .05$.

10:10 AM—Break from Classes, Check Facebook, Text Friends
10:20 AM—Back in the Classroom (Biology Lab)

In highlighting the apolitical classroom experiences of most high school and college students, we are not suggesting that schools do not attempt to raise civic awareness through government and US history classes. Indeed, many young people mentioned voter registration drives at school, as well as school administrators and teachers who encouraged them to vote and to follow the 2012 presidential election. A few college students even reported that they had professors who canceled class on Election Day not only so that the students could be sure to cast a ballot, but also so that they could volunteer on a campaign if they were interested. But even with these broad attempts to infuse civic and political engagement into secondary and postsecondary education, politics is peripheral for most students throughout their high school and college years.

Consider the messages that young people receive—or don't receive—from their teachers and professors. One-third of high school and college students said that a teacher or professor served as an important mentor in helping them think about their future and what career they might pursue. Apart from parents, these are the most influential adults in young people's lives. Yet only 12 percent recount any sort of encouragement from these mentors to consider someday running for office.[15] As with parents and other adult family members, the educators in young people's lives do not push them toward a future in politics. This is not surprising in light of the low regard most adults have for politicians (see Table 3.3). It may also explain the assessments offered in a 2013 MIT Center for Civic Media presentation, in which a group of scholars and activists concluded that teachers and educational reformers increased civic participation dramatically since the 1960s, but had not done the same for political engagement.[16]

12:20 PM—Lunch, Two Conversations via Text Message, Watch
   YouTube Video
1:05 PM—Final Class of the Day (Pre-Calculus)
2:25 PM—Soccer Practice

Young people's disengagement from politics at school tran-
scends the classroom. We asked the students we surveyed whether
they participated in 16 popular extra curricular activities. Most reported being active in several groups and clubs. Half participated
in some sort of community service or volunteer organization, and
many spent time in music/band, church or religious groups, and
organized sports. The fact that volunteering and community service were the most popular on the list speaks to a recurring theme
in this book (and one that we discussed in chapter 2): Young people
want to improve the world and their communities, but they tend
not to think of politics as an effective means to do so. Just look
at the results in Table 4.2. Of the activities we listed, three could
be considered political: student government, debate team/mock
trial, and College Democrats or Republicans. Of these three, only
one—student government—made it into the top half of the list
(still with less than a 20 percent participation rate). Debate team/
mock trial and College Democrats or Republicans placed 14th and
15th, respectively.

3:05 PM—Quick Break from Sports Practice, Text Friends about Get-
   ting Together
4:00 PM—Update Facebook Status, Yearbook Committee Meeting
4:30 PM—Head Home, Hang Out with Friends (Discuss Crushes
   and Weekend Plans)

The typical high school or college student spends quite a bit
of time socializing with friends. Among the young people we

surveyed, 55 percent said that they had a regular group of friends and 39 percent reported spending time with multiple groups of friends. Only 7 percent did not spend time with a consistent group of people outside of school. Much like their school and extracurricular experiences, though, young people's friendships tend to be pretty devoid of political content.

Table 4.2 Young People's Participation in Extracurricular Activities

Community service or volunteering club	50%
Music / Band	40
Church or religious group	40
Organized sports outside of school	35
Varsity or junior varsity sport	32
Honor society	29
Drama / Theater club	24
Student government	**18**
Fraternity or sorority	15
Yearbook club or committee	15
School newspaper	14
Pep squad, cheerleading, drill team	13
Intramural sport	12
Debate team / Mock Trial	**12**
College Democrats or Republicans	**12**
Academic club (math, writing, etc.)	9
N	4,280

Notes: Entries indicate the percentage of respondents who have participated in each activity. Data for fraternity or sorority participation, as well as for College Democrats or Republicans, are restricted to the 2,117 college students in the sample, since these are not activities available to high school students.

We asked the students what subjects they discussed with their friends, and how often they talked about each topic. Figure 4.1 presents the percentage of people who discuss each topic with their friends at least every week. School was the most popular topic of conversation, followed by music, food, and movies and television. Current events, in general, ranked toward the bottom of the list, behind dating, family, and sports. And, by today's standards, talking about current events does not connote a discussion of world politics or public affairs. It was clear in our interviews that for today's young people, "current events" often include the latest Kardashian marriage, the release of a new Taylor Swift song, or whether it's going to rain on Friday. Politics came in dead last as a topic of conversation, with less than 20 percent of young people reporting that they had even one recent political discussion with their friends.

Figure 4.1 Topics Young People Discuss with their Friends

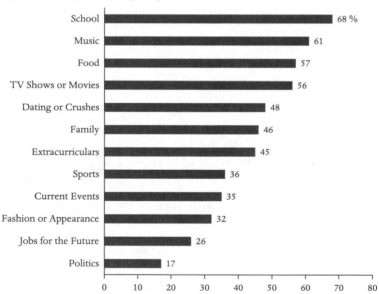

Notes: N = 4,208. Bars indicate the percentage of respondents who discuss each topic with their friends weekly.

These findings are consistent with the annual UCLA higher education survey conducted with incoming first-year students.

In recent years, roughly 20 percent of college students report frequently discussing politics with their friends.[17] Our results also exemplify a shift from previous generations. More than one-quarter (27 percent) of the young people we surveyed said that they never talk about politics with their friends. This is almost double the percentage from the 1970s.[18] The low levels of political discussion we uncovered are even more striking given that we carried out the survey in October of a presidential election year, a time when it is often difficult to avoid news and conversations about politics, campaigns, and elections.

We saw the same pattern in our interviews when we asked young people about how frequently they discuss politics or current events with their friends. Although a few of the high school and college students said they talked about politics regularly, the vast majority (94 out of 115) did not. As Charlotte, a high school junior who "hangs out with friends, like, every day after school," put it, "Politics is just not what we're interested in. We're into music and what's happening at school, and also activities after school, stuff like that. That's what's interesting." Jake, also a high school junior, doesn't discuss politics with his friends either. Instead, he and his friends "talk about movies, sports, you know, things that are fun and interesting." Tracy, an aspiring artist at a college in New England, commented, "My friends just aren't crazy into politics. They know more than I do, but even for them, it's not their focus. We are more into talking about art, music, life." It is quite easy to assemble from the interview transcripts a list of similar comments:

> Do my friends care about what's going on in the world? I don't know . . . No they probably really don't. (Amber, high school freshman)

> Most of my friends are apathetic and don't know what is going on. (Anna, high school junior)

Politics is boring. And we are in high school, so we really can't do anything about it. (Gabriel, high school senior)

Most of my friends are big-time texters. They don't care about things outside the texting world. They're just doing that. But that's what younger people do. We just don't care about politics. We focus on other things. (Rebecca, high school sophomore)

We don't care at all about current events and politics. . . . This era is full of people who don't care about anyone else. (Derek, high school junior)

I just don't talk about politics too much. It doesn't ever come up. It doesn't interest my friends. Maybe when we get older, it will be interesting. (Megan, college sophomore)

For many young people, asking if they talk with their friends about politics was a little like asking if they ever talk about lawn bowling or traveling to Antarctica. The topic is utterly obscure.

When we turned specifically to the 2012 presidential election, young people were more likely to acknowledge the importance of keeping up with politics and discussing it with their friends. But they still demonstrated a deep ambivalence or disinterest that often kept them from having political conversations. Julian, for example, is a literature major at a university in Kentucky. Most of his friends are English majors, too. He explained that, in general, they "just didn't care about the election." He did feel guilty about it, though: "We know it's important, but it is just so hard to force yourself to watch news about politics. There's so much else that's more fun and interesting. I guess we should all be ashamed." Alyssa, a criminal justice major from Arkansas, wished that she and her friends cared about politics more: "This was the first time we could vote, so I wish we wanted to follow the news more. But most of us don't pay attention a lot. We are torn because we know we should care, but it's really hard to see why." Caesar, a high school senior from Georgia, was a little less circumspect in his comments: "No one I talk to cares about politics. It's boring and really removed from our lives."

5:45 PM—Homework
6:30 PM—Dinner with Family (and Not Talking about Politics)
8:00 PM—Chilling with a Favorite Device (Watching Pretty Little Liars, Texting Friends about It)

The Internet and social media are more than just a mode of communication and source of information for young people. According to a 2012 Aspen Institute poll, 59 percent of young adults believe that the Internet greatly influences their sense of right and wrong.[19] Despite the importance young people accord to digital technology, or how easy it makes it for them to access information about current events and politics, today's young people tend not to encounter much news through these devices. We asked whether, in the last few days, they got news from 10 different sources. The most popular source of information remains television; almost half of the people surveyed reported watching a traditional news broadcast—such as those on ABC, CBS, or NBC—at least once in the last few days (see Table 4.3). Facebook and Twitter came in second, confirming that young people rely on social media for news. As far as other media are concerned— online newspapers, political websites, and political blogs, all of which have proliferated in the last few years—most high school and college students do not visit them at all.[20] Nor do they tune into *The Daily Show with Jon Stewart* or *The Colbert Report*.

These political satire programs might be amusing and influential for the 13 percent of young people who watch them on a regular basis. But they have limited power over the 87 percent who rarely or never do.[21]

Table 4.3 Young People's News and Media Habits

In the last few days, did you get news from . . .	
Broadcast television (such as ABC, NBC, or CBS)	45%
Facebook or Twitter	37
Cable television (such as Fox News Channel, CNN, or MSNBC)	33
News browser (such as Yahoo, MSN, AOL, or Google)	30
Radio	22
YouTube videos	21
Online newspaper or political website	18
Hard copy newspaper	16
The Daily Show with Jon Stewart or *The Colbert Report*	13
Political blog	7
N	4,280

Notes: Entries indicate the percentage of respondents who report accessing news through each source.

Our survey results are similar to a 2012 Pew study that uncovered major generational differences in the amount of news people consumed, regardless of the source. The "Silent Generation," which includes people over the age of 65, spent, on average, 84 minutes watching, reading, or listening to the news the previous day. Baby boomers (people between the ages of 48 and 65) consumed a little less, but not much: 77 minutes' worth. Generation X-ers absorbed about 10 minutes less news each day than their parents. But the real drop off was among millennials. On average, they consumed only 46 minutes of news the previous day. The "truly troubling trend for the media," according to Pew, is that there is no reason to believe that news consumption increases as people get older. The trends for each generation were flat; people in 2012 consumed approximately the same amount of news they did eight years earlier.[22]

The story is much the same when we focus specifically on the types of websites young people visit at least a few times a week. More than three-quarters regularly use the Internet for social networking, listening to music, and watching YouTube videos. But less than half visit news websites on a regular basis, and only about one-quarter scan political websites consistently. Shopping, sports, entertainment, and celebrities are just more interesting and appealing (see Figure 4.2). Again, these low numbers for politics are probably higher than usual given that we conducted the survey in the weeks leading up to the 2012 presidential election.

Figure 4.2 Types of Websites Young People Visit

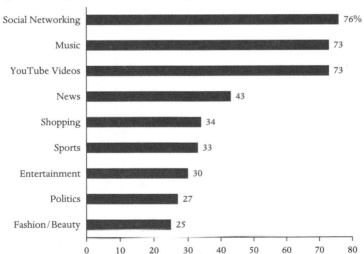

Notes: N = 4,222. Bars indicate the percentage of respondents who visit each type of website "a few times a week" or "every day."

The fact that students do not access much politics online is reinforced by the messages they receive about how they should use their mobile devices. A *Buzzfeed* list of "18 Apps Every College Student Should Download Right Now," for instance, does not include any mention of news or current events. Rather, college students are encouraged to download Clear, which helps them sync their to-do lists from multiple devices; WaterIn, which helps them track how much water they should drink based on the amount of alcohol they've consumed; SleepCycle, which tracks REM cycles; and 7 Minute Workout, so as to avoid the "Freshman 15."[23] *Mashable*'s "List of 25 Apps You'll Need to Survive College" also lacks any mention of a source for news or current events.[24] As does its list of "10 Must Have Apps for Successful High School Students."[25]

> 11:00 PM—*Final Facebook Status Update, Last Text Message Conversations for the Night*
> 7:12 AM—*Wake Up, Check Facebook, Text Three Friends*

How Contemporary Politics Leads Young People to Avoid It

Today's young people are not politically engaged. To be sure, some of this detachment results from the fact that they think news, current events, and world affairs are boring and irrelevant. As the results in this chapter have already made clear, some segment of high school and college students today have almost no opinions about politics or politicians because they have never actually contemplated these topics. Overall, this group constitutes about one-quarter of the young people we surveyed and interviewed. But much of the political disengagement we uncovered is far more deliberate. Through our interviews, we learned that many young people—roughly 60 percent of them—avoid politics on purpose. They have opinions about politics, most of which are decidedly negative. Accordingly, they rationalize their political disengagement because what they know about politics (even when it's often very little) is so unappealing and frustrating that they shut it out of their lives.

And who can blame them? We live in a time where almost all national news about politics is negative and combative in tone. It is almost as though there is no longer any place for thoughtful journalism or positive news coverage of politics. When it comes to measured and fact-based news, political scientist and media scholar Thomas Patterson concludes, "Journalists are failing to deliver it."[26] Instead, contemporary politics in the United States is presented as a constant stream of scandal, conflict, and failure. When *Time* magazine identified the top ten overall news stories of 2013, for example, five were political, and they all painted the US government in a very negative light: the IRS and Benghazi scandals, the government's failure to secure gun-control legislation, the government shutdown, the troubled launch of the Affordable Care Act, and the travails of NSA whistleblower Edward Snowden.[27] CNN and NBC deemed the 16-day government shutdown and the flawed rollout of Obamacare the top two political stories of the year.[28] And when media outlets are not highlighting Washington's inability to get the job done, they are featuring political coverage that often amounts to partisans from both sides of the aisle predictably condemning one another. In early 2014, for example, the Fox News Channel regularly treated its audience to a hyperbolic presentation of stories about Democrat Barack Obama's "failed policies," whereas its liberal counterpart, MSNBC, gleefully aired an endless series of stories lambasting the Republican-controlled House of Representatives for its inaction and obstructionist tactics.

It's not only television news that presents politics as ineffective. Late-night comedians reinforce these messages by pointing out the many ways that Washington is broken. On a nightly basis, anyone flipping through the channels can hear about the latest political failure. Consider the way Jon Stewart described Congress in a July 2011 episode of *The Daily Show*: "I'm not saying this Congress is bad at its job. I'm just saying that this Congress is equivalent to a skunk with its head in a jar of Skippy peanut butter." When House Republicans held their 33rd vote to repeal the Affordable Care Act, then–*Late Night* host Jimmy Fallon, in July 2012, joked, "It was mostly a symbolic vote that accomplished nothing—or as Congress calls that, a vote." President Obama's push for Congress to raise the minimum wage in February 2013 led Jay Leno to tell his *Tonight Show* viewers, "Believe me, when it comes to doing the minimum for their wage, Congress knows what it's talking about." These characterizations are by no means atypical. On any given night, a viewer can enjoy a wide range of political humor that condemns Washington:

> Today the Senate swore in a record 20 female Senators. Yep, the women said they're very excited, and look forward to proving they can accomplish just as little as male Senators. (Jimmy Fallon, January 2013)

> A top geneticist at Stanford says human intelligence is declining. You know what that means? We are seeing Congress at its smartest and most effective right now. (Jay Leno, February 2013)

> Tomorrow President Obama gives his annual State of the Union address. If you're not familiar, the State of the Union is where the president faces Congress and asks them to work together and fix America's problems and Congress says, "No." (Jimmy Fallon, February 2013)

A petition to have Justin Bieber deported got over 100,000 signatures, which means the White House now has to legally rule on it. So finally a chance for Obama to issue an executive order that both Republicans and Democrats can agree on. (Jay Leno, January 2014)

Last night of course was the State of the Union address. President Obama promised to focus on economic growth, education, and healthcare. Or as people tuning in put it, "Oh crap, it's a rerun." (Jimmy Fallon, January 2014)

And the list goes on and on.

The laughable, tragic, and upsetting way that the mass media portray politics was reflected in two broad themes that came across in our interviews. Because young people perceive government, current affairs, and the political system as (1) confrontational, and (2) ineffective, they choose to sidestep conversations about it and minimize its presence in their day-to-day lives. This behavior is particularly acute among the younger generations. National surveys find that, whereas 58 percent of people who are 48 and older report that they enjoy following the news a lot, only 29 percent of millennials do.[29]

Why Would I Want to Argue with My Friends?

When young people today look at Washington, DC, they are confronted with a partisan, conflict-ridden environment. And as we discussed in chapter 1, national politics is the lens most people use to evaluate the political system. So, as news and political information have become more partisan, so has the discourse used by many of the adults in young people's lives. Today's high school and college students infer, therefore, that any and all political discussion is contentious and ugly. Thoughtful debates over important issues of the day and calm conversations regarding campaigns and elections are alien propositions. When they are with their friends, young people don't want to argue; they'd rather get along and have fun.

For some of the people we interviewed, the tendency to avoid politics was a lesson learned from previous experience. Stephanie, a high school senior who wants to major in business, is interested in politics. After some "heated discussions" about the 2012 presidential election, though, she started to avoid political conversations with her friends:

> We talked about the presidential election at the beginning and it became pretty obvious that my friends and I did not agree on who we wanted to win. When we realized that we had drastically different ideas, we decided that it would be best not to talk about it anymore. There's no reason to fight.

Gavin, a high school senior, recounted a similar course of events. He told us that he and two of his closest friends used to talk about politics from time to time. But it became clear that they had "lots of opposing views." Although Gavin acknowledged that "sometimes, it's fun to have some debates," he concluded that "it's not very good to disagree so much." It got to the point that talking about politics was "just not pleasant." Justin's experiences were much the same. The high school junior noted that he and his friends would "occasionally" talk about politics and current events. But they found themselves disagreeing and arguing so much that they decided it would be best "to enjoy the time [they] spend together and talk about fun stuff."

Most of the young people we interviewed, though, never actually had political conversations with their friends. Many anticipated that it would not go well, that they might disagree, so they avoided the topic altogether. Aaron, a high school senior who plans to major in math when he gets to college, considers himself "very interested in politics." But when he is with his friends, he tries to "stay away from politics," because "talking about it is a really easy way to get into a fight and lose friends." Keith, a college freshman, agreed:

> I don't know why I'd want to talk about politics with my friends. It can change friendships. You know, I don't want it to get too heated. So, maybe we can sometimes talk about current events, but I'll never talk to my friends about the parties and that sort of stuff. I think I have an idea of what side my friends are on, but I'm not sure. And I try not to let them know my views.

The potential consequences also keep Nicole from talking about politics with her friends. According to the 21-year-old communications major, "Talking about politics would mean having disputes. What friends want to do that? We try to avoid those. With friends, you try not to be confrontational, not stir the pot." Ashley, a college senior from Los Angeles, elaborated on the ramifications of raising political issues with her friends:

> If I bring up anything more specific than a simple political fact—like, hey, Obama won the election—my friends are like, 'I don't follow.' And then that makes me want to tell them that this is our country and that they should care. But then they'll think I'm being antagonistic, so I don't do it.

For Catherine, a high school senior who took a government class last year, talking about politics "leads to too much drama." She described her friends as "very opinionated. They punish people with different views." Julian summarized this line of reasoning best when he said bluntly: "Nope, we never bring it up. Politics kills the mood."

I'd Like to Care, but It's Just So Broken

Beyond wanting to avoid confrontation, high school and college students perceive the political system as so broken that they are not interested in following it closely. In fact, their general impressions do not sound that different from those offered by evening news anchors or late-night comedians. Lizbeth, a geography major, told us that when she thinks of Congress, "the word *stuck* comes to mind." Erin, a high school senior, felt the same way: "At the highest levels of politics, everything is just gridlocked. It's so bad and it feels like there is nothing anyone can do to fix it." Mary, an education major who hopes one day to teach history, offered a similar evaluation: "The government is not effective, no one can agree on anything, so nothing of any significance gets passed. It's depressing to follow. So, I don't." Kelly, a physical education major, agreed:

> I don't like the system. It doesn't work. You have all of these people in politics who have to vote along a party line. . . . But you should be able to vote differently if you want to. Otherwise, you can't get anything done if the parties are split. I'd like to care, but I just can't. I can't watch it. It's ridiculous. It's broken.

Many young people perceived politics as a series of pointless conflicts and stubborn refusals to cooperate. Shauna, an 11th grader, recalled a class project that required her to track a piece of legislation as it tried to make its way through Congress. The assignment led her to conclude that Congress is ineffective: "Ugh . . . there are lots of times when Congress just doesn't want the president to have anything good on his record, so they stall or won't do anything. And that's really frustrating because it's not what they're supposed to do." Calvin, a high school sophomore, also thought that partisanship resulted in nothing but problems for the government: "People in Congress argue all the time. They support policies that are really inefficient, but they can't agree on anything big or important." He said that what they are able to accomplish "just isn't that important," so he tends "not to follow it that much." The "constant fighting," coupled with the fact that "the system is so corrupt," has led Joshua, a business major in his first year of college, "to turn it off completely. I'm not interested in politics anymore." Bryce, a biochemistry major who hopes to pursue a career in the health-care field, might have summed up best how the political system functions—or doesn't: "The government is run by children. They are little kids. They always bicker and nothing substantial seems to get accomplished."

From the perspective of the young people we interviewed, the perceived ineffectiveness in Washington is not the only reason they turn away from politics. Many are also disgusted with the electoral process, explaining that modern-day campaigns are "horrible," "dumb," and "almost impossible to watch." As Dylan, a nursing major, commented, "Elections are about mudslinging and people bring up irrelevant issues that should not matter." Emma, a criminal justice major, articulated a similar view:

> Elections are just too nasty and they touch on subjects that we probably should not discuss. Like when Obama was running and they brought up things about his past and Donald Trump said that he'll donate money if Obama shows his birth certificate. C'mon. I used to like watching scandal stuff sometimes, but this has just become so stupid.

Mikayla, a double major in visual arts and public health, explained that she does not like the invasiveness of modern campaigns:

> The loss of privacy if you are running for office is just terrible. I don't like how they bring things up from your past and put

them into the public. . . . These things don't matter for whether you're fit to be in office. They're really stupid things to bring up. I'm not going to spend time on that.

Hadleigh noted that she is not interested in following the news because "the system right now has all of these people who really focus on pushing projects for their specific area so they can win their elections. They're always focused on the wrong things." It's for much the same reason that Holly, a college junior, "doesn't think much about politics." The education major explained that politicians "will do whatever it takes to get re-elected, and that means that they're not interested in anything other than votes. That's not interesting to me. It makes me angry actually."

These negative attitudes about campaigns and elections came through in dozens of the interviews, indicating that young people find the electoral process so distasteful that turning away feels like the only sensible reaction:

> I think the mudslinging has gotten worse over the years. I guess it is because society changes and that's what works. I'm not going to watch it, though. (Gavin, high school senior)

> Elections are too nasty. They're basically a gladiator match. It's pointless to watch. (Latrell, high school senior)

> Campaigns are so awful. I get so frustrated with the way they go back and forth, and I can't tell who is telling the truth. Everyone just supports their own party. Sometimes it's, like, what is the point in following this? (Aliza, high school senior)

> In a campaign, you make a little mistake and it gets blown up. The commercials blow up everything. Things that aren't even mistakes get blown up and words are always miscon-strued. Or they cut things in an incorrect manner. It's not true

usually. So, what's the point of following the election? (Anna, high school junior)

I don't like following elections. I don't trust politics. And when you don't trust people or like what they do, it is hard to want to know about it. (George, college junior)

Shauna, the high school student who had to track the piece of legislation for a school project, put it most colorfully when she concluded, "I hate that elections are usually about choosing the shiniest of two turds."

The Consequences of Limited Political Exposure

Young people's limited exposure to politics and current events does more than tell us that they are not fully aware of what's going on in the world around them. It also affects their political ambition. High school and college students who do not know about or care about politics do not aspire to hold office in the future. On the other hand, when young people's daily lives include at least some exposure to politics—even though the political environment is extraordinarily negative—they are far more likely to consider running for office.

The data presented in Figure 4.3, along with our interviews, make this clear. The figure provides examples of how the different ways that politics makes it into young people's daily lives can influence their interest in running for office. For instance, a young person who takes a political science course in college or a government class in high school is almost twice as likely as one who doesn't to express interest in running for office (14 percent compared to 8 percent). As Aaron, a high school senior, explained, "I really got into politics this year with one of the government classes I took." Through the class, he learned that running for office could be "an interesting way to change the community." Aaron's teacher also played a vital role: "My teacher got me thinking about it. He was really inspiring and a really cool guy. His devotion to the class and the way he explained things, that really helped me think about what I might want to do later."[30]

Figure 4.3 School, Peers, Media Habits, and Young People's Political Ambition

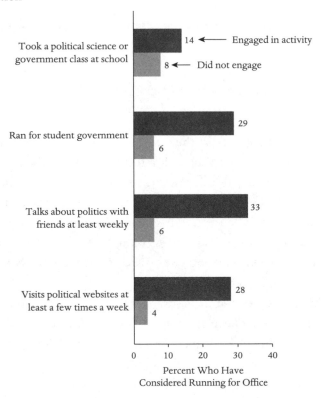

Notes: N = 4,277. Black bars indicate the percentage of respondents who have considered running for office and engaged in the activity. Gray bars indicate the percentage of respondents who have considered running for office, but have not engaged in the activity. The ambition gap is statistically significant at p < .05 in all comparisons, with respondents who have engaged in each activity more likely to exhibit political ambition than those who have not.

High school and college students who participate in political extracurricular activities are also far more open to running for office later in life. Those who ran for a student government position, for example, are five times more likely than those who did not to express interest in a future candidacy. Indeed, for Tony, the decision to run for class representative in ninth grade opened his eyes to the world of politics: "I was not the most active kid in school, but when my friends and teachers encouraged me to run for class rep, I did it and I won." Now a senior in college, Tony plans to go to law school and believes running for office someday "just might be in the cards." Jason, a college senior majoring in business, first became interested in running for office when he was in junior high. His school ran a mock presidential election in 2004, and he "loved it." Soon after, Jason starting telling friends that his initials "stood for the branches of government: judicial, executive, and legislative." Since then, he has "always thought" that he'd ultimately run for office.

And young people who regularly visit political websites or spend time with friends who discuss politics are dramatically more politically ambitious than those who do not. Russell is one of these high school students. He told us that hanging out with his friends sustains his interest in politics:

> My friends and I are kind of the geeks at school, always walking around talking about the death penalty or global warming or who is going to be president. It makes me follow the news a lot so I can keep up. We're always online finding out the latest. It kind of makes me want to maybe be in politics someday.

Louise, a college sophomore, also attributed her political ambition to her friends: "They made me think about running someday. After they told me I should, I kept thinking about it. It's nice to know that my friends think I have good ideas and know what I'm talking about. That just inspires me to want to be a leader."

The importance of regular exposure to politics is even clearer when we consider the joint effects of different types of exposure. Consider the four examples we provide in Figure 4.3: taking a political science or government class, running for student government, talking to friends about politics at least weekly, and visiting political websites on a weekly basis. The young people we surveyed had anywhere from zero to four of these experiences. Only 2 percent of those who "scored" a zero ever considered running for office. Among high school and college students who scored a two—let's say, they took a government class and regularly discussed politics with their friends—17 percent considered running for office. At the other end of the spectrum, 60 percent of the young people who scored a four were open to running for office. The problem, of course, is that only 2 percent of the students we surveyed scored a four.

The patterns are similar when we look at high school and college students separately. The main difference, as we discussed earlier in this chapter, is that high school students are less likely than college students to be exposed to politics. Among the college students, 4 percent reported experiences consistent with all four activities included in Figure 4.3. Only 1 percent of high school students did. But the magnitude of the relationship between political exposure and political ambition is the same for both groups of students.

Importantly, even among the small group of young people who were open to running for office someday, decidedly negative views of the political system prevailed. Shauna, an 11th grader who could "certainly imagine" serving in Congress someday, characterized contemporary politics this way:

It all seems so corrupt in Congress. . . . I wish they would be more direct. . . . And the political parties? Oh my God. I hear fights about it on television between the parties all the time. And we discuss it in my house. I'll never understand them. They separate our country too much.

Maddie, a college junior, was also enthusiastic about the prospects of running office someday. Although she thinks it would be "amazing to be an elected official in Congress or something like that," she "wouldn't want it to be like the way politics is today. They don't get anything done and fight all the time. I see that everywhere. But it would be a great thing to do." Those people who can stomach the negativity and dysfunction are more politically ambitious as their exposure grows. The problem is that most young people shy away from that exposure, in large part because of the negativity and dysfunction.

Conclusion

When Georgetown University students enroll in classes each semester, they have an opportunity to take "Women in American Politics," a course taught by Donna Brazile. The adjunct instructor managed Al Gore's presidential campaign in 2000 and serves as the vice chair of Voter Registration and Participation at the Democratic National Committee. But every Wednesday, she leaves behind Washington politics, enters the classroom, and teaches about the "history of women in the political process and the hard fought battles they've had to wage over many decades." According to Ms. Brazile, teaching is "one of the most important things" she does every week.[31]

Since she began teaching 20 years ago, Ms. Brazile has mentored countless students. Beyond helping them master the course material and secure internships and jobs on political campaigns, she thinks it is her responsibility to encourage students to become politically active and engaged, especially female students: "Women in politics need to become more visible in the political landscape to encourage the next generation of female leaders. Visibility is viability. Young girls need to see female leaders, to be able to envision themselves in those positions."[32] She believes that teaching provides her with "another platform to reach the next generation waiting in the wings."[33]

The evidence presented in this chapter demonstrates the power that direct mentorship and encouragement in an educational setting—much like Ms. Brazile provides—can have on young people. But our survey results and interviews reveal that, for most young people, day-to-day exposure to politics is limited. Although school provides the opportunity for students to focus on politics and world affairs, they don't. This holds true whether we are talking about curriculum and substantive content, classroom discussions, or the messages transmitted by most teachers and professors. Young people tend only to encounter politics when they enroll in a government or political science class; for most students, this is only one class in one semester of either high school or college. When they move from the classroom to their afterschool activities or to the couch in front of the TV, most high school and college students continue to experience politics only peripherally. We live in an information age that facilitates the transmission of data and ideas, but the next generation is not interested in using these resources to learn about politics or keep up with the world around them.

In examining the reasons for young people's political disinterest and disengagement, the state of contemporary politics plays a substantial role. Young people navigate a culture in which national politics—their primary lens for evaluating the political system—is portrayed in the news almost universally as ineffective, hyperpartisan, gridlocked, and conflict-ridden. And where the news leaves off, political satirists like Jon Stewart and John Oliver, and late-night comedians such as Jimmy Fallon, Jimmy Kimmel, and Conan O'Brien, pick up with jokes about political ineptitude and incompetence. Is it really a surprise that most of the high school and college students we interviewed who had something to say about politics said something very negative? More surprising would be if they didn't.

The irony, of course, is that when young people are exposed to politics—even the negative, disconcerting aspects of it—they are much more open to a political future. When their friends are interested in politics, when they take government classes they like, when they use the media to stay informed about news and current events, they are more ambitious to rise up and become political leaders. When young people are deeply immersed in politics, they push through their initial revulsion and see a way to contribute. The current political system is just so off-putting that very few young people expose themselves to politics in the first place.

5

I'm Not a Corrupt Liar Only Out
for Myself: I Could Never Run for Office

On August 8, 2008, John Edwards sat down in his North Carolina living room and gave an exclusive interview to ABC's *Nightline*. The Democratic Party's vice presidential nominee in 2004 and a presidential candidate in 2008, Edwards was in damage-control mode amid allegations of adultery and the misuse of campaign funds to cover up the affair. The scandal initially struck many Americans as pretty far-fetched. Edwards was known for his doting and loving 30-year marriage to his wife, Elizabeth, who was battling cancer. According to journalist Bob Woodruff, the relationship highlighted the couple's commitment to Democratic causes and showcased "the determination of Elizabeth Edwards to devote the last years of her life to her husband's ambitions."[1] But when the *National Enquirer* released in July 2008 damning photographic evidence of the affair and a child Edwards reportedly fathered, the mainstream media could not ignore the story. And Edwards himself was left with little choice but to respond.[2]

Early in the *Nightline* interview, Edwards admitted to, and apologized for, his relationship with Rielle Hunter. But he rubbed people the wrong way when he noted that the affair began when his wife was "in a period of remission from cancer," that he "welcomed the opportunity to participate in a paternity test," and that he had "no awareness" of the misuse of campaign funds to cover up the matter. He later admitted that he is, in fact, the father of his former mistress's baby.[3] And although a jury deadlocked and the prosecutor decided to drop the case, Edwards was indicted for misusing $1 million in campaign contributions to hide the affair and Hunter's pregnancy during the 2008 race for the White House.[4]

Even if he did not use the interview to tell the truth to the millions of Americans who had followed his campaign, Edwards did seize the opportunity to explain his behavior:

> I grew up as a small town boy in North Carolina. You know, came from nothing, worked very hard, dreamed that I'd be able to do something hopeful and helpful to other people with my life. I became a lawyer. Through a lot of hard work and success, I got some acclaim as a lawyer. . . . Then I went from being a young Senator to being considered for vice president, running for president, being a vice presidential candidate, and becoming a national public figure. All of which fed a self-focus, an egotism, a narcissism, that leads you to believe you can do whatever you want. You're invincible, and there will be no consequences.

In offering this justification, Edwards confirmed many of the stereotypes that people have about politicians.

Edwards' conduct might have been particularly egregious, but we need to look no further than to the last few years to assemble a list of elected officials who lied to cover up their own misdeeds. In many cases, the deception was so transparent that the politicians had no choice but to exit the political arena. Eliot Spitzer, for example, stepped down as governor of New York in 2008 when a federal wiretap revealed that he patronized an escort service (ironic, given that, as attorney general, Spitzer prosecuted several prostitution rings).[5] Anthony Weiner resigned from the US House of Representatives in 2011 when the cyber evidence made it impossible for him to continue to deny that he used Twitter to send nude images of himself to a woman who was not his pregnant wife.[6] That same year, Christopher Lee, who represented an upstate New York district, gave up his congressional seat when *Gawker* released shirtless photos he sent to a woman with whom he was seeking a relationship on *Craigslist*. The 47-year-old married congressman described himself on the site as a 39-year-old divorced lobbyist who was a "fit, fun, classy guy."[7]

Although Spitzer, Weiner, and Lee stepped down when their scandals exploded, in many cases, politicians behaving badly suffer little in the way of a penalty, perhaps because this kind of behavior has become run of the mill. When it came to light in 2007 that US Senator David Vitter frequented a Washington, DC–based escort service, he apologized for his "serious sin," said that he made peace with his wife, and paid virtually no price at the polls.[8] Or consider former South Carolina Governor Mark Sanford's escapades. In June 2009, Sanford "went missing"; neither his wife nor his staff knew his whereabouts, as he had abandoned his security detail and turned off his cell phone.[9] Upon his return, Sanford initially said he was hiking the Appalachian Trail. He later admitted to visiting a woman in Argentina.[10] Despite disappearing from the state for nearly a week, Sanford completed his term as governor. Three years later, he sought the seat he previously held in the US House of Representatives. Newly divorced, Sanford claimed a 10-point margin of victory in the race, his Argentinian fiancé at his side.[11] (The relationship ended in September 2014, when Sanford took to Facebook and broke up with the woman in a 2,346-word status update.[12])

Of course, bad behavior comes in many varieties. Beyond lying and adultery, today's politicians engage in routine hyperpartisanship, name-calling, and obstructionism. Representative Steve King, a Republican from Iowa, dug in his heels in 2014 over immigration reform and challenged Democratic US Senator Chuck Schumer to a duel over "who actually has the xenophobia."[13] Then-Senate Majority Leader Harry Reid, frustrated by the millions of dollars the Koch brothers have infused into Republican campaigns and super PACs, resorted to ad hominem attacks on the Senate floor. He called the conservative pair "about as un-American as anyone" he could imagine.[14] US Senator Ted Cruz epitomized the unwillingness to compromise that characterizes Washington politicians when he spearheaded the 2013 government shutdown in an attempt to defund the Affordable Care Act. The problem, of course, even according to many of Cruz's Republican colleagues, was that he offered no plan to reopen the government.[15] Basically, he shut it down because he could; Senate rules and norms empower individual senators to wreak havoc single-handedly if that's what they want to do. Although immigration, campaign finance, and health care are all topics worthy of serious debate and deliberation, thoughtful discussion and progress are often subsumed by provocation and histrionics.

It has even reached the point where elected officials on both sides of the aisle are criticized when they exhibit just the slightest willingness to seek middle ground. The Charleston County Republican Party, for instance, censured US Senator Lindsey Graham for "not being Republican enough."[16] He earned this distinction despite receiving a lifetime score of 88 (out of 100) from the American Conservative Union.[17] But what could he expect after supporting President Obama's Supreme Court nominees and working with Democrats on immigration reform? John McCain received a similar censure from the Arizona Republican Party, which condemned his "long and terrible" record of voting with liberal Democrats to end the government shutdown and to bring to a vote an amendment that would expand background checks to guns purchased at gun shows.[18] The Tea Party Patriots, an organization fighting for limited government, called Republican Speaker of the House John Boehner a "tax and spend liberal" when he worked with Democrats to end the government shutdown in 2013.[19] Liberal bloggers berated Democratic Congressman David Cicilline for "refusing to stand up for progressive values" when he cooperated with Republicans and mainstream Democrats to reduce the deficit.[20] And the *Daily Kos,* a popular left-wing blog, referred to moderate Democrats as "a pile of suck."[21] These dynamics leave today's elected officials with little incentive for any sort of bipartisan cooperation.

In this day and age, it is easy to eye-roll or yawn as stories of political misdeeds, infighting, and refusals to compromise pop up on the computer monitor, television, or smart phone. But the fact that these episodes now seem typical does not make the politicians who engage in them any less narcissistic, rash, or stubborn. It does not mean that public policy does not suffer when elected officials cannot work together. And it does not inoculate citizens against developing political attitudes based on this behavior. In fact, political scientists have provided compelling evidence that political scandals and politicians' misdeeds—from marital infidelity to tax evasion to lying under oath—can affect citizens' overall evaluations of government and politics, often driving down their political trust.[22]

By no means do we suggest that most politicians behave this way. But as we demonstrate in this chapter, the most appalling and ugly behavior of today's politicians deeply influences young citizens' views of political leaders. Given the media's propensity to cover scandal and conflict throughout the 24-hour news cycle, the lens through which young people evaluate politicians is often shaded by reckless and irresponsible conduct, an ardent unwillingness to compromise, and condemnation of those who do. Even though many young people want to be leaders and believe that they have the characteristics and experiences necessary for these roles, they do not associate the positive leadership traits and skills they possess and value with those they see in politicians. Rather, they are so turned off by contemporary political leaders that they have no aspirations to join their ranks. These negative attitudes toward candidates and elected officials serve as our third explanation for young people's low political ambition.

Young People's Perceptions of Contemporary Politicians

Every year, Gallup polls a national sample of Americans to find out who they most admire. It's an open-ended question, so people can name anyone they have "heard or read about, living today in any part of the world." Presidents usually take the top spot, but the percentage of people who name the president has decreased considerably in the last 60 years. In 1955, President Eisenhower topped the list, with 26 percent of those polled offering him up as the man they most admire. By the time Bill Clinton earned the title in 1996, he did so with the support of less than half that proportion, as did George W. Bush when he won the honor in 2007. Barack Obama's "Most Admired Man" status was conferred in 2013 by only 16 percent of Americans.[23]

Unfortunately, Gallup has not polled teenagers and young adults on questions like this. But the limited evidence that does exist suggests that, across generations, admiration for politicians has decreased over time. In 2010, for example, Ronald Riggio, a professor of leadership and organizational psychology, asked a group of his students which leaders they most admired. He found that the majority identified family members and people they knew personally. This struck Riggio because, previously, most students in his classes chose historical and political leaders, or sports and media figures"[24] The sentiments of Riggio's students, however, are consistent with recent national polls of young people. When asked to identify their heroes, 50 percent of 13–24 year-olds in an Associated Press/MTV poll named a parent; the rest mentioned other family members, friends, God, and an occasional teacher or professor. Political leaders did not appear anywhere on the list.[25] Even when young people are asked to name role models other than their parents, politicians fare poorly; they lose out to other family members, friends, teachers and coaches, religious leaders, entertainers, and athletes.[26] In November 2012, when YPulse revealed the results of a poll that asked millennials to name the "top influencers" of their generation, only one political leader—Barack Obama—even made the list of dozens of names. And he was ranked as far less important than, among others, Mark Zuckerberg, Lady Gaga, Justin Bieber, Selena Gomez, and Taylor Swift.[27]

Why don't politicians occupy more slots in young people's "most admired" lists? Why don't they achieve "role model" status? Why aren't they the next generation's "heroes?" The answer is actually pretty simple: from the perspective of young people, there's very little to admire. As part of our national survey, we asked whether a series of descriptions applied to political leaders in general. Four of the statements were positive, such as "they are smart and hardworking" and "they are willing to stand up for what they believe." The other four statements were negative, including "they are only out for themselves" and "they are argumentative."

(Table 5.1 lists all eight statements.) The results are what we would expect given the examples that opened this chapter. Only a small proportion of survey respondents believed that the four positive statements accurately describe contemporary politicians. Less than one-quarter considered politicians interested in wanting to help people, and even fewer thought that politicians stand up for what they believe. The negative statements, on the other hand, struck a chord with roughly twice as many high school and college students, who were far more inclined to perceive today's political leaders as argumentative and dishonest than as smart and hardworking. Our results are consistent with a recent Harvard University Institute of Politics poll of young adults: roughly 60 percent of 18–29 year-olds report that "elected officials seem to be motivated by selfish reasons."[28]

Table 5.1 Young People's Attitudes toward Politicians

When you think about political leaders in general, do you think they are . . . ?	
Positive Attributes	
Willing to stand up for what they believe	27%
Smart and hardworking	21
Interested in wanting to help people	15
Ordinary people	12
Negative Attributes	
Dishonest	42
Happy being the center of attention	38
Argumentative	38
Only out for themselves	36
N	4,280

Notes: Entries indicate the percentage of respondents who reported that the phrase accurately describes most politicians.

Not only do young people hold political leaders in low regard, but they are more likely to do so now than in the past. In the 1970s, about 55 percent of high school seniors agreed that "almost all people in government know what they are doing."[29] Compare that to the mere 21% of young people we surveyed who think that most political leaders are smart and hardworking. More than half of that same group of high school seniors in the 1970s trusted government to do what is right at least most of the time, and more than one-third thought that public officials really cared about the people they represented. Fast-forward to our 2012 survey, and only 15 percent of high school and college students think that politicians are interested in helping people.[30]

The interviews we conducted provide more depth and nuance for assessing attitudes about today's politicians. We sought to give young people ample opportunity to express what comes to mind when they think about political leaders, and we wanted to do so without suggesting that they consider any specific attributes or traits. So, in the interviews, we asked what they think of politicians generally, how they feel about the president and members of Congress, whether they think politicians are effective at their jobs, and whether they admire people who run for office. Although our questions did not intend to solicit any particular type of response—they were entirely open-ended, and answers could go in any direction—about two-thirds of the people we interviewed offered negative comments and impressions.

Some of the things we heard were amusingly inaccurate. One young man, for example, was concerned about "the people" on Capitol Hill: "From what I understand, most members of Congress have a criminal record and should not be there." Another bemoaned the "fact" that "most people in politics have been there for 50 years. They're trying to drag us back in time and they don't understand anything." A high school sophomore characterized all politicians as part of the "super rich." She told us that she heard that "they are all millionaires and billionaires doing whatever they can to make even more money." A college freshman explained that "the excessive salaries" are a problem "because people in politics do so little." From what she gathered, "members of Congress are lazy and always on vacation. They are never doing any work in Washington." While these statements clearly embody and exaggerate the worst clichés Americans hear about politicians, the earnestness in how they were conveyed to us illustrates young people's willingness to believe and relay almost anything negative about political leaders.

More prevalent than these outlandish and exaggerated negative assertions about politicians, though, were dozens of comments that shed light on why young people hold political leaders in such low regard. These attitudes—which we break down into three broad categories—are both predictable and discouraging. In many ways, they also cut to the heart of our central argument: young people perceive contemporary political leaders so negatively that the thought of possessing the traits they think politicians exhibit turns off the next generation to a future of political leadership.

Me, Me, Me . . . That's All They Care About

Empathy and a desire to act in the interests of the people are among the most important qualities citizens look for in their leaders.[31] The notion that today's representatives try to do the best they can for their constituents does not jibe with young people's perceptions, though. The political leader as a servant of the people is an entirely foreign concept. Rather, young people believe that politicians care little about anything or anyone other than themselves:

For the most part, I don't admire politicians. They are out for themselves. They want to advance their own careers. (Rafael, college junior)

Most politicians are hypocrites. They are two-faced. They will say one thing to get elected and then turn around and do what is in their best interest. (Dilery, college sophomore)

Overall, I think most politicians are kind of secretive. . . . I don't think they think about the majority of Americans. They just think about themselves. (Alexis, college senior)

They seem like they are usually out for themselves. They don't seem to care about regular people. (Hayden, high school junior)

Politicians I usually think are out for themselves. I've not really seen any politicians who care. They normally just do what they want to do. (Sam, high school sophomore)

The quest for more power, more money, and more prestige drives politicians' behavior; a sense of empathy does not.

For many people we interviewed, these general characterizations of self-interest were rooted in their sense of politicians' desire for reelection. Juan, a junior in college, epitomized this view: "Congress is filled with old men who are getting very little done. . . . They are just self-interested incumbents who are constantly worried about reelection." Or as Mikayla, a college senior, put it, "All they care about is their careers, which means doing whatever it takes to get elected and then reelected." Both of these students also mentioned that lost is the goal of "working for the people" or "doing what would be best for the people."

But many of the students were far more cynical; they believed that politicians are corrupt and use their positions not to secure their political future, but to advance their own financial well-being. Jack, a communications major, stated matter-of-factly, "A lot of politicians are just in it for the perks and the money." Fabio, a college freshman who aspires to be a lawyer, issued a far more serious indictment: "Many politicians are sleazy businessmen who put on a front. Their whole life is just a façade. All they care about is money. They are just trying to get rich." Cam, a nursing major, agreed. He thinks that most political leaders "want to help their own businesses and those of their friends. You know, give them a leg up." Nicole's detailed assessment of how you get to Congress in the first place highlights the communication major's sense of the role that self interest plays in the process:

> I think a lot of them are just socially forced into the job. Their parents were rich and in politics and wanted to advantage their own businesses. So their sons are supposed to do the same thing. I think politics is somewhat closed to the general public; it's more of a family business. Rich families have rich kids who run for office. And then those kids make the families even richer through their own political positions.

Even several young people with little interest in politics held deeply negative impressions of politicians, describing them as "only out for themselves," "totally self-interested," and "selfish and not at all effective." Mark, an electrical engineering major, captured the self-interest theme particularly well when he said that politicians are only there "to figure out how to make money for themselves. It's like, me, me, me. That's all they care about. It's not about the voters or the people they're supposedly representing."

Who Cares What They Say? It's Probably Not True Anyway

Examinations of effective leadership tend to identify open and honest communication as a key ingredient.[32] And most research that examines the traits that are important to citizens when they evaluate candidates includes integrity among the top four.[33] But this is not what young people see or hear. In fact, one of the most common themes to emerge from the interviews has to do with political leaders' lack of integrity.

Many young people made it clear that they simply do not believe anything that politicians or elected officials say. Leon, a criminal justice major, explained that he does not like politicians because of "all the lying and empty promises." Vivian, an English major in her junior year of college, agreed. She does not think politicians listen to people. Instead, she explained, "They lie. It's like they pretend they listen, and they say they are going to do something. But then they surprise you and don't do it." She then paused and added, "Well, I guess that is not a surprise at this point." Overall, 57 of the 115 people we interviewed expressed concerns and, sometimes, even disgust about politicians' widespread dishonesty, as the following list of quotations makes clear:

> I think there's too much lying in politics. (Jessica, college sophomore)

> Politicians have to lie all the time. That is what politicians do. I think everyone who runs in an election is a lying sack of shit. Politicians just suck. (Derek, high school junior)

> In my opinion, I don't know how to put it, exactly. Politicians are just liars. Sometimes, it sounds like they are lying all the time. (Jeffrey, high school freshman)

Most of them lie—all they say is lies. (Shawn, high school senior)

The thing that bothers me about politicians is the amount of lying that goes on. Everybody lies. It seems like people in higher places in politics seem to lie constantly to get out of situations. I don't admire politicians. (Becca, high school sophomore)

The most unappealing thing about members of Congress is that they are corrupt and always trying to win over crowds. They do it by being deceitful. If you become a politician, you have to be comfortable being dishonest. (Catherine, high school senior)

The president and Congress, they are a bunch of liars. They think they're more important than everyone else and they lose touch. (Charlotte, high school junior)

Martin, an 11th grader, summed up for many young people a troubling consequence of distrust toward political leaders: "When you don't believe the president or the other leaders out there, you just end up tuning them out. Who cares what they say? It probably is not true anyway."

The Job Made Them Do It

When John Edwards linked his adultery and deception to a system that feeds politicians' egos and hubris, he articulated a widespread perception about the political system—one that emerged very clearly in our interviews: politicians engage in dishonest, self-interested behavior because the broken, flawed political system encourages it. The young people we interviewed did not simplistically argue that politicians are bad people doing bad things, but rather, offered more thoughtful evaluations of why politicians behave dreadfully.

Perhaps the best way to illustrate this point is by recounting a series of conversations we had with students who explained how elected officials evolve from good, selfless people into corrupt liars. Anjelica, a college student from California, considers herself "pretty aware" of politics and current events. When we asked for her overall impressions of politicians, she said that "they start out effective, but then they change." We asked her to elaborate. How do they change? What makes them change? She laughed and said, "The best way to put it? They are ridiculous! That's really the best way to describe them: ridiculous and self-centered. They probably had good intentions at the beginning, but the system feeds their egos, it makes them do bad things." She almost made it sound like a forgone conclusion: "They start out effective, but down the line the little devil takes over." Then there's Samantha, a liberal arts major at a college in the northeast. She explained that "most politicians, if you boil it down, have a good heart. But they get lost being politicians." When we pushed her on what she meant by "being politicians," Samantha told us that "they are too busy trying to please everyone. But they don't really have a choice. That's what they need to do to succeed in politics. The way the system works makes it impossible for politicians to stay good people." Abby, who plans to study entomology when she begins college, also attributed her negative attitudes toward politicians to the system: "The people themselves in politics are pretty good at the beginning, but then they have to sell out if they want to get anything done. Then they don't seem so good anymore."

Navigating a system that "is full of dirty money," "turns a blind eye to corruption," and "makes it easy to cover things up" appears to do more than encourage bad behavior, though.

According to many of the students we interviewed, it actually rewards it. Several young people mentioned, for example, that candidates who raise the most money tend to win. Many of the same people also noted that the money politicians raise often "has strings attached," "is dirty," or "is like a bribe." "But what are they supposed to do?" asked Eliza. "Not take it? Then they'll be out of a job." Others referred to politicians spending all of their time with other politicians, wealthy donors, and "people who want something from them." Consequently, Sarah, a college junior, explained, "They don't really know what a normal life is like anymore. But they must still make laws for the everyday citizens. Of course they don't know how to do that." Matthew, a high school junior, summed it up by chronicling what happens to people when they spend too much time working in a broken system: "Even the nicest people, when they become politicians, get to be pretty corrupt and lose their genuine feelings for helping others. They lose their honesty as well. It's like they have no choice." Matthew views the power of the system as so strong that it's the reason he doesn't want to go into politics: "I don't want to be like that, become corrupt and care only about myself. It's like the job made them do it. I don't want that to happen to me."

Negativity clearly pervades young citizens' attitudes toward politicians. Although some of the people we surveyed and interviewed seemed to have no impressions of political leaders (this group of individuals was truly disengaged), the majority expressed a general distaste for them. This is important for two reasons. First, it discourages young people from feeling any kind of connection to their government. Second, as we show in the remainder of this chapter, it deters young people from being motivated to work in what they perceive as broken, dysfunctional political institutions with dishonest, corrupt politicians.

No Leadership Deficit: Young People's Assessments of Their Leadership Traits and Skills

How does someone become a leader? What makes a good leader? Scholars have long debated these fundamental questions. For the first half of the 20th century, most examinations of leaders were predicated on the notion that certain innate characteristics are responsible for great leadership. But the modern study of leadership has evolved to the point that most scholars acknowledge that both character traits and situational factors influence leaders' emergence. Indeed, political scientists Thomas Cronin and Michael Genovese identify four phases in the learning of leadership, two of which are early childhood development, and education and growth. They argue that most people with leadership abilities develop and hone these skills through a series of life events and practices.[34] Styles and types of leaders differ widely—from the great charismatic personality to the quiet, effective facilitator—but the acquisition of key leadership traits and skills tends to start relatively early in life.

This is definitely true for the young people we surveyed. They have clear ideas about what leadership means to them, and many have substantial leadership experiences under their belts. More than one-third held a leadership position in at least one extracurricular activity; one in five had leadership positions in multiple organizations (see Table 4.2 for the list). As far as typical leadership attributes are concerned, they have those too. We asked about eight traits (see Table 5.2). Roughly three-quarters identified themselves as friendly, and a similar proportion considered themselves smart. More than four in ten reported that they are confident, competitive, and/or ambitious. Overall, more than 60 percent of the young people we surveyed thought they had at least four of the eight traits we listed. They also demonstrated a willingness to embrace different life experiences that might afford them opportunities to be leaders. A majority of the students were not only open to trying new things, but also recounted regular success when they embark on new endeavors (see bottom of Table 5.2).

Table 5.2 Young People's Self-Perceived Leadership Traits and Skills

Traits	
Friendly	81%
Smart	74
Confident	53
Attractive / Good looking	49
Cooperative	48
Competitive	44
Ambitious	43
Assertive	26
Attitudes and Skills	
I am generally pretty good at most things I do.	62%
I am usually willing to try new things.	61
I often have new ideas about things I want to do in life.	51
I am a good writer.	42
I am good at speaking in front of people.	29
N	4,280

Notes: Entries indicate the percentage of respondents who self-assess as possessing each trait or characteristic, or who said that the sentence accurately described them.

In discussing their leadership experiences, however, a clear mismatch emerged between young people's ideas about what a leader is and their perceptions of how politicians behave. This disconnect surfaced as soon as we asked whether and why they considered themselves effective leaders. Many shared with us well-thought-out ideas about how they became good leaders. Bryce, for instance, is a chemistry major in college. He considers himself the leader of his lab group and the "person people come to when they have questions." He attributed his leadership skills to playing football: "In high school, I was the defensive captain on the football team. This experience really helped me become a leader. I always knew more than my teammates because I thought a lot about what we needed to do to succeed." Jack, a communications major, who "always tends to be the project leader for groups at school," explained that his leadership abilities evolved from his participation in extracurricular activities. He "started out slow, as a member of a community service group." When he first joined the group, Jack said that "everyone would just argue." He became more involved and realized he had a knack for "stepping in and getting everyone to work out their differences." For Jessica, being the oldest of four siblings helped her develop confidence as a leader. The sophomore French major recalled "always organizing and directing [her] kid brothers." She was often in charge, and that gave her a feeling that she was "good at running things." Bryce, Jack, and Jessica's experiences are typical of those of the young people we interviewed; those who considered themselves leaders pointed to their relationships with family members, friends and peers, or teammates as fundamental building blocks that allowed them to cultivate their leadership abilities. The pivotal experiences that lead young people to think of themselves as leaders are rooted in teamwork and compromise, neither of which featured prominently, if at all, in their descriptions of politicians.

The incompatibility between young people's perceptions of effective leadership and what they think of politicians also shone through when they mentioned the traits that make them good leaders. For many students, "people skills" and the "ability to listen" topped the list. Calveon, a high school senior who hopes to pursue a degree in business when he gets to college, commented, "I am a good leader in social situations. I'd describe myself as energetic, outgoing, and fun loving. I am able to lead because I understand what others want. I hear what they say and I act accordingly." Jana, a high school senior who aspires to be a doctor, feels comfortable taking the lead in most group situations because she listens carefully:

> I always try to listen to people and try to understand them. I am always taking other people's thoughts into account. That really helps for bringing people together and solving problems. It seems like now, being in charge and running things seems to just happen naturally.

Franklin told us that he typically takes on leadership roles in academic group projects. The college sophomore considers himself successful because he "can listen well, identify the strengths of others, relate to everyone, and delegate." Being "a good listener" and "communicating to others what they need to do" were also at the top of Kristen's list of reasons she thinks she is an effective leader. Fittingly, the sophomore communications major concluded that "communication really is the key to being a good leader."

The majority of people who considered themselves leaders also referred to their impulse to help people and foster a sense of cooperation. Joshua, a business major, said that he "goes into leadership mode" whenever he sees that "someone needs help." His desire to help others, he explained, is rooted in his background playing sports: "The coaches always tried to instill leadership in us and teach us how to help the younger kids. I guess that stuck." Thomas, a college junior who has held leadership positions in several school clubs, "likes being a leader" because he "feels good helping people succeed." For Alexis, a social work major, being a good leader means "trying to help everyone do better." She learned this lesson as the captain of her high school dance team. Because the competition was team-based, not individual, she realized, "It was not all about me. What was important was trying to lead in a way that was best for everyone, best for the team."

Beyond good communication skills and a desire to help people, high school and college students noted several specific skills and traits that contributed to their leadership success:

> I'm really charming. I can talk to anyone I see on the street. It's really easy for me to be a leader. (Thomas, college junior)

> I'm a go-getter. My parents taught me to be ambitious. If you see a problem, you should try to solve it. (Vivian, college junior)

> Decisiveness. That's what makes me a good leader. I make decisions and then go from there. I feel like a lot of people tend to waver and cannot make decisions. I am not like that. (Adam, college sophomore)

> I'm a good leader because I'm a smart jock. I've always been good at sports, but I'm good at school, too. People respect people who know what they are doing. (Eugene, college senior)

> Being a quick thinker is really important since the people you lead will look to you to solve the problems. (Seth, high school senior)

> It's about honesty and integrity. I am a successful leader because I say what I mean and I do what I say. People have to believe you to follow you. (Leon, college sophomore)

Others identified themselves as "collaborative," "open-minded," "willing to compromise," "good planners," and "effective problem-solvers" when asked about their leadership qualities. In the end, almost two-thirds of the young people we interviewed said they believed they had at least some of the traits and qualities of good leaders.

Young people see themselves as leaders, possess many leadership skills and traits, and articulate well-conceived ideas about what effective leadership entails. Their descriptions of what the word "leader" means, though, certainly do not conjure up the images of politicians they described earlier.

The Relationship between Attitudes toward Politicians and Political Ambition

The disconnect between leadership and politics is important because it bears directly on political ambition. Our survey results indicate that approximately 60 percent of young people believe that when they finish school and have been working for a while, they will know enough to run for office. But the overwhelming majority—many of whom are bright and driven—would never in a million years think that the political arena would be a place to showcase their talents and abilities. This came across in several of the interviews.

Consider Evan, a smart, talkative 10th grader who described himself as "very excited to improve the world." Our conversation made it clear that Evan sees neither his ambitious behavior nor his desire to better society as an indicator that he should consider running for office. In fact, he considers politics anathema to his long-term goals, in large part because the traits and characteristics he thinks are important for good leadership tend to be absent from the politics.

Question: Do you consider yourself a good leader?
Evan: *Yes. I am the senior patrol leader of my Boy Scout troop. I have always been somewhat of a leader. I like being a leader. I like having people looking up to me. I like trying to help people.*
Question: How do you think you got to be a good leader?

Evan:	Good parents and good teachers showing me the way. Listening to everyone and being confident in myself. Not always being too strict.
Question:	Would you ever consider running for office in the future?
Evan:	No. I would never want to run for office. People tend not to like you no matter what you do. It does not even feel like most politicians are leaders. They are always fighting with each other, not helping the people who need it.

Our conversation with Julius, a high school senior, was similar:

Question:	Do you consider yourself a good leader?
Julius:	Yes, I am destined to be a leader. I often take on leadership roles in academic clubs. I also lead a music group.
Question:	How do you think you got to be a good leader?
Julius:	I am able to identify the strengths of others. I also know when to delegate and when to ask for help. It's also important to be able to identify a problem and quickly identify a solution. People you lead will look to you to solve problems. I am very confident in my ability to fix things.
Question:	Would you ever consider running for office in the future?
Julius:	Would I ever run for office? Probably not. I have the knowledge. If I wanted I could definitely be the next POTUS or Senator. But people in politics are usually out for themselves. I just don't think much of politicians and Congress. I'm not like that.

Instead, Julius hopes to put his penchant for leadership to use by becoming an engineer who "helps design cities and transportation systems."

Like Evan and Julius, Amelia expressed confidence in her leadership skills, but quickly wrote off any interest in running for office. The college sophomore, who is majoring in the humanities, perceived a blatant incongruity between the leadership qualities she thinks are useful and important and those that the political system rewards.

Question: Do you consider yourself a good leader?

Amelia: *I'm a pretty good leader, I guess. I am the VP of Students Against Destructive Decisions. And I'm the youngest shift manager at my job. I'm also the oldest in my family, so I help out my younger brothers a lot. Next year, I'm going to run for office of my chapter of the National Honor Society.*

Question: How do you think you got to be a good leader?

Amelia: *I'm confident in the things that I do. So, if I have an opportunity to lead, I take it. I don't take control and I listen to others. I like to lead with more of a collective strategy than a strict hierarchy. And I'm not bossy, so people generally like me.*

Question: Would you ever consider running for office in the future?

Amelia: *No, I'm not cut out for Washington. I think politicians are unsavory characters. I'm not interested in watching people play politics. They're all about the words, but we all know that actions speak a lot louder than words. I think they're out of touch when it comes to all of these economic loopholes for wealthy people. I think getting into office is just about having the money and getting power. Their values are different than mine.*

Finally, Sheila is a first-year college student majoring in biology. She, too, is a proven leader, but eschews any notion of running for office.

Question: Do you consider yourself a good leader?

Sheila: *Yes, I'm a good leader. I led a lot of clubs in high school. I really liked my leadership roles. They were a lot of fun.*

Question: How do you think you got to be a good leader?

Sheila: *I think I'm good at leading because I hear people, I think about what they have to say, I am not just trying to get to do what I want. I am fair and willing to compromise when I work with people.*

Question: Would you ever consider running for office in the future?

Sheila: *I don't see myself ever running for office in the future. I like leadership roles, but politics is not what I want to do in life. Everyone I know says politicians are corrupt.*

As these interview excerpts illustrate, many high school and college students cannot conceive of how they could possibly apply their knowledge and leadership skills to politics. Our survey results indicate, for example, that only 13 percent of high school and college students who identify themselves as confident are open to running for office in the future. Just 12 percent of young people who think of themselves as competitive are politically ambitious. Strikingly, only 13 percent of young people who consider themselves "ambitious" report interest in being a political leader.[35] They tend not to see in politicians any of the qualities they see in themselves that make them successful and effective.

But the flip side is also true. The small percentage of high school and college students who view contemporary political leaders favorably—often as possessing the positive leadership traits they see in themselves—are much more likely than those who don't to express interest in running for office. Figure 5.1 illustrates this relationship. The black line shows that young people's political ambition increases as they associate politicians with more positive traits. Only 8 percent of young people who did not associate political leaders with even one of the positive descriptions we offered are open to a future in politics. Young people who believe that all four descriptions generally apply to politicians are three times as likely to be politically ambitious.

Figure 5.1 Assessments of Politicians and Young People's Political Ambition

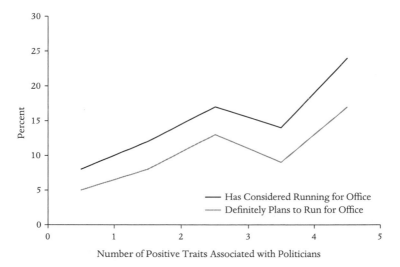

Number of Positive Traits Associated with Politicians

Notes: N = 4,280. Lines show the relationship between young people's positive evaluations of politicians and their interest in running for office. The relationships are statistically significant at p < .05, with more positive assessments corresponding to greater levels of political ambition.

The relationship is just as powerful when we examine whether high school and college students have a "definite" interest in running for office. As the gray line in Figure 5.1 indicates, fewer people fall into this category overall, but "definite" interest correlates with positive attitudes about political leaders. Of course, only 3 percent of the young people we surveyed associated all four positive descriptions with politicians (compared to 57 percent who did not think that any of the positive statements applied).

In light of the negativity most young people relay about politicians and the political system, who are these strange individuals who assess political leaders so favorably? Why do they offer such positive evaluations? They are the rare few who navigate highly politically charged environments—so much so that they gain exposure to more than superficial characterizations of the US political system. They take government and political science classes, run for student government, talk about politics with their friends, and consistently watch and read political news. Young people who engage in all four of these activities are 11 times more likely than those who engage in none (11 percent compared to 1 percent) to associate all four positive traits shown in Table 5.1 with politicians. They are also only approximately half as likely (36 percent compared to 67 percent) to offer no positive assessments of politicians whatsoever.

At first glance, the notion that more political exposure is associated with positive assessments of politicians might seem to fly in the face of our central argument. Wouldn't these young people be the most turned off because they see the most negative aspects of politics more often? Not quite. It is true that the most politically exposed are more likely to associate politicians with at least one negative description. More specifically, 78 percent of young people who have taken a government class, run for student government, talk about politics with their friends at least weekly, and visit political websites on a regular basis offer at least one negative evaluation of political leaders. This is significantly greater than the 67 percent of high school and college students with none of these experiences who offer at least one negative assessment.

But their heightened levels of exposure also increase the likelihood that they will encounter competing examples and a more nuanced view of politics. Along with the lying and the cheating, they see some politicians passionately advancing a cause. They encounter local and state politics, which tends not to be as mired in gridlock and ineffectiveness as national politics. And they come to understand that the broad brush of scandal and corruption does not apply in every case.

Daniel's experiences are useful for elaborating on this logic. The engineering major who plans to pursue a master's degree and teach science is very interested "in someday running for a state or local position." He doesn't see politicians through rose-tinted glasses, though, telling us that "at least 50 percent of them are not very good people." He went on to say, however, that "the rest are decent and trying to do a good job." Later in the interview, Daniel shared with us that he is a big news consumer and regularly reads *The Atlantic*, *The Economist*, and *Foreign Policy* online. (He was the only one of the 115 people we interviewed to identify serious news sources among his favorite websites.) Daniel noted that they have taught him that "everything is not so clear cut when it comes to politics."

Sadie's story is similar. A sophomore psychology major, she thinks "it is really critical to follow the news." But a cursory glance is insufficient. Sadie explained, "Sometimes, you have to wade through a lot of negative stuff to stay informed and figure out what is what." Though she is "skeptical of the intentions of most political leaders," she also "sees a lot of good people working really hard." Sadie is open to the idea of running for office, and thinks "it might happen" after she "gets her career going." For every Daniel or Sadie, though, 10 young people are so turned off by their limited exposure to politics that, rather than wade through the muck to develop a more nuanced, multi-faceted assessment of politicians, they rely on their negative impressions and dismiss a political future altogether.

A Note on Race: Barack Obama and Young People's Political Ambition

Any assessment of young people's political aspirations must take race into account. After all, elite-level politics remains a business dominated by white men, and the limited inclusion of traditionally marginalized groups has been relatively recent and slow-going. Douglas Wilder, of Virginia, served as the first elected black governor, but that was not until 1989.[36] Only eight African Americans have served in the US Senate since Reconstruction, and two of them were appointed to fill vacated terms and were not reelected. New Mexico's Susanna Martinez and Nevada's Brian Sandoval are the only Latino governors. And although the first Hispanic governor served as early as 1875, only 11 Latinos have ever been chief executive of a state.[37] Only four Latinos serve in the US Senate, and three of them were elected after 2007. Blacks and Latinos are significantly underrepresented in the US House of Representatives and in state legislatures across the country, too. Roughly 8 percent of members of the US House of Representatives are black and 7 percent are Latino or Hispanic. Among state legislators, slightly more than 8 percent are black and just less than 3 percent are Latino or Hispanic.[38] We raise these issues here because the presence of traditionally marginalized groups in positions of political power can signal that the political system is open and inclusive. In addition, this kind of group consciousness can stimulate voter turnout and political activism, as well as result in greater substantive representation of black and Latino constituents' interests.[39]

Our survey results suggest that a shared racial identity also appears to be linked to the race differences in political ambition we uncovered in chapter 2. Turning once again to the four positive descriptions of politicians we asked our survey respondents to consider, black high school and college students were almost 30 percent more likely than white students to associate at least one positive trait with politicians. They were more than twice as likely to think that politicians generally possessed at least three of the four positive traits we listed. The pattern among Latinos was similar, albeit a bit less pronounced.[40]

Racial differences are just as marked when we focus on politicians' negative traits: they are only out for themselves; they are happy being the center of attention; they are argumentative; and they are dishonest. Whereas 77 percent of white high school and college students associated at least one of these negative descriptions with today's politicians, only 56 percent of black and 64 percent of Latino students did. White students were also more than twice as likely as black students and 40 percent more likely than Latino students to believe that all four negative descriptions apply to contemporary politicians.

What is the root of these disparate assessments? The survey results suggest that attitudes toward Barack Obama have a lot to do with them. We included on the survey a question that asked young people whether they felt at all inspired by four politicians: Barack Obama, Hillary Clinton, Sarah Palin, and Mitt Romney. Obama and Romney, of course, were running for president at the time of the survey; and Clinton and Palin were the highest-profile women in politics. We present the results in Figure 5.2. Overall, 75 percent of black students, 51 percent of Latino students, and 45 percent of white students considered at least one of the four politicians an inspiration. Two findings stand out. First, Barack Obama far surpasses the other political figures as inspirational. Second, his appeal is particularly strong among black students (70 percent report being inspired by the president). Obama's appeal extends to Latino respondents as well; they were considerably more likely than whites to consider the president inspirational.

Figure 5.2 Political Figures Young People Find Inspirational

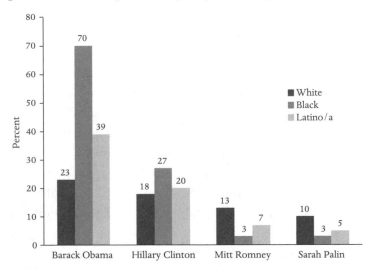

Notes: N = 3,823. Bars indicate the percentage of respondents, within each race, who identified the political figure as inspirational. The gaps between black, white, and Latino respondents are statistically significant at p < .05 in all comparisons except for the differences between whites and Latinos' evaluations of Hillary Clinton and blacks and Latinos' evaluations of Sarah Palin.

Because young people who are inspired by a particular politician are more inclined to evaluate all politicians favorably, positive attitudes toward President Obama play an important role in shaping black and Latino respondents' overall assessments of political leaders and the government. In the Obama era, black and Latino adults are also about twice as likely as whites to trust the federal government. According to a 2013 Pew poll, 38 percent of blacks and 44 percent of Latinos, compared to 20 percent of whites, "trust the government in Washington to do what is right" either always or most of the time. [41] As we've made clear throughout this book, these more positive attitudes toward politicians and the political system bear directly on political ambition.

This came through in the (albeit limited number of) interviews we conducted with students of color. Emma, a criminal justice major, enthusiastically told us what the Obama presidency means to her: "Barack Obama has opened a lot of doors for people. I think being a leader is something for kids to shoot for. And now it seems possible in a way that it wasn't always for everyone." Having "watched all that Obama has been able to do," Emma said that she would "definitely consider" running for office. She'd even "love to be President someday." Richard, a high school junior, also linked his political ambition to President Obama. Not only did he first start following politics in 2008 when he realized that "Obama actually had a chance to win," but he also started thinking about his own political aspirations at that time: "I saw what he did and I thought, yeah, I'd like to be president. I'd like to be like Obama. He's a good leader. Obama and his wife are both great leaders. I'd like to help people the way they do." James, an undeclared major in his second year of college, was even more direct. He explained, "As an African American, Obama has made me feel like I can accomplish anything." Although James does not know for sure whether he will ever run for office, he believes that the opportunity is now his to seize: "With Obama there, I know that I could run if wanted to."

Conclusion

At a recent speech at the University of Texas, Chelsea Clinton, the 34-year-old daughter of former president Bill Clinton, lamented that none of her friends—"smart" and "accomplished" people— would ever consider running for office. She contrasted this reality with her father's years as a student at Georgetown in the 1960s, when "about half of his classmates were pondering a future in politics."[42] Our survey responses from thousands of young people shed light on at least part of the reason for Chelsea Clinton's observation. Although many young people aspire to be leaders, most have a very negative view of politicians. They do not associate their own leadership attributes with political leadership, and they have no desire to enter the fray.

Given some of the egregious behavior of today's politicians—behavior that high school and college students have been exposed to consistently their entire lives—it's hard to blame them. For many of the young people we interviewed, the earliest political memory they could recount was a dishonest president. For some, that president was Bill Clinton, who looked the American people in the eye, wagged his finger, and famously proclaimed, "I did not have sexual relations with that woman, Miss Lewinsky." Clinton eventually admitted to the affair with Monica Lewinsky.[43] For even more young people, the dishonest president they first remember is George W. Bush, who many perceived as leading the country into a war with Iraq on the false pretense that Saddam Hussein had weapons of mass destruction. Throw in decades of hyperpartisan responses to presidential dishonesty, a litany of high-profile political scandals, and frequent examples of political corruption, and it is hard to imagine why any young person would view politics in a positive light.

And there is likely no end in sight. We remain more than a year away from the 2016 presidential election, but criticisms, allegations, and innuendos about potential candidates are well under way. Democratic frontrunner Hillary Clinton is already being attacked by her opponents on multiple fronts: she's too old, she has lied about her health, she was an incompetent and deceptive secretary of state. Republican strategist Karl Rove even suggested that she might have "brain damage."[44] In recounting Clinton's three days in the hospital for a blood clot that resulted from a fall, Rove took some liberties and accused Clinton of misleading the American public: "Thirty days in the hospital? And when she reappears, she's wearing glasses that are only for people who have traumatic brain injury? We need to know what's up with that."[45] New Jersey governor Chris Christie, a leading Republican potential candidate for president, has been embroiled in what has become known as "Bridgegate," in which his administration allegedly created massive traffic jams in Fort Lee, New Jersey, by closing several lanes at the toll plaza of the George Washington Bridge.[46] Political opponents argue that the lane closures were meant to punish Fort Lee's mayor for not supporting Christie's reelection bid. In a similar vein, Hoboken mayor Dawn Zimmer accused the Christie administration of withholding Hurricane Sandy relief from her city unless she approved a real-estate development project.[47] Keep in mind that Clinton and Christie have yet to decide whether to run for president.

Certainly, politics in the United States has long been a nasty business. We can find examples of outrageous rhetoric and offensive allegations dating back to the first contested presidential election. In 1800, Thomas Jefferson accused President John Adams of being "a hideous hermaphroditic character," while Adams characterized Jefferson as "the son of a half breed Indian Squaw."[48] Until the early 1990s, though, no readily accessible media outlets made it their 24-hour-a-day mission to tear down the president or chronicle the misdeeds of a political party. We now live in a time, and young people have grown up in an era, in which negative information about our political leaders is everywhere—on talk radio, on the Internet, on television. The negativity is so ubiquitous that even young people who avoid political news pick up snippets of politicians' dishonesty, self-interest, and corrupt behavior second hand, often from friends, parents, and teachers, or while surfing the Internet. These morsels leave a sour-enough taste in high school and college students' mouths that they are turned off to politics and would never consider running for office.

In light of the fact that politicians have little incentive to change their behavior, and the all-encompassing news media will remain motivated to bring us every detail, where does this leave us? What, if anything, can be done to inspire future generations to take up the mantle of political leadership? This is the topic to which we now turn in the final chapter of this book.

6

Inspiring the Next Generation to Run for Office

I think the way to make politics more appealing in general is to be honest about what's at stake. Not talk around the subject. Not a lot of gobbledygook, but just simple, straightforward talk. And I think that will cut through the cynicism that so many young people have. But I also think more young people running for office, at the city council level, at the board of supervisor level . . . More young people running will have an impact on other young people. And I encourage it.

—Senator Barbara Boxer, *in a video for Generation 18, an organization that tries to spur political activity in young people.*[1]

I know that many of you are here today because you are passionate about public service and want to make a difference in public policy. So I am here to tell you that I wholeheartedly encourage you to get out there and run yourself. Run yourself! Don't look to the person next to you or down the street or that leader that you thought was a really good speaker. Look within you. Don't let anyone tell you that you're too young to make a difference or that it's best to wait your turn.

—Congresswoman Debbie Wasserman-Schultz, *at the 2012 Campus Progress National Conference.*[2]

I encourage more young people to run for office, just as I did. I will be the youngest member of Congress when I take the oath on January 3rd. Whether it's on the local, state, or federal level, our voices need to be a part of the conversation. . . . You do not need a long political resume, just a love of country and deep desire to make our government work better for the people.

—Congressman Patrick Murphy, *in an interview with MTV in 2012.*[3]

More than two centuries ago, the US government was founded on the premise that elected leaders be drawn from the ranks of regular citizens. James Madison believed that it would be best if elected representatives were "men called for the most part from pursuits of a private nature, continued in appointment for a short time."[4] George Mason argued in favor of the citizen legislator when he said, "Nothing so strongly impels a man to regard the interest of his constituents, as the certainty of returning to the general mass of the people, from whence he was taken."[5] And, weary of hereditary succession and monarchical rule, Thomas Paine highlighted the ills of a ruling class when he wrote that "men who look upon themselves born to reign, and others to obey, soon grow insolent . . . and are frequently the most ignorant and unfit of any throughout the dominions."[6] Since the time of the founding, a central philosophy underpinning the US political system is that citizens should step forward and run for office.

The tradition of calling on Americans to engage the political system and become political leaders has continued throughout US history. Perhaps most notably, President John F. Kennedy, in his inaugural address, famously urged people to "ask not what your country can do for you, ask what you can do for your country."[7] His call to service inspired thousands of Americans to seek local, state, and federal office. (And, in the case of Bill Clinton, even the presidency.) On the Republican side of the political spectrum, President Ronald Reagan's emphasis on "preserving freedom" and "limiting government" had a similar effect.[8] US Senator Ted Cruz remembers being just 10 or 11 years old when Reagan turned him onto a life in politics: "If you look at the leadership style of many of the new leaders who are rising up, it is a generation that was raised on Reagan. . . . When we were coming of age, we had the most extraordinary example of how to be."[9]

Although current politicians continue to encourage young people to consider a career in politics—as the quotes that opened this chapter indicate—the message does not seem to resonate. After spending a year surveying and interviewing young citizens, consider what we learned:

- Very few young people have any interest in running for office when they get older. Nearly nine out of ten say they will not even consider the possibility.
- Most families do not prioritize politics. And on the rare occasions when they do talk about politics, conversations are often contemptuous and focused on government ineffi-ciency and politicians' ineffectiveness.
- At school, with friends and peers, and through the media, young citizens try to avoid exposure to politics. When they do encounter it, what they see and hear tends to be negative, confrontational, and divisive.
- When young people think about effective leadership, poli-tics does not come to mind. They are so turned off by politi-cians that running for office does not occur to them as a way to apply their leadership abilities.

With more than half a million elected positions, the US political system will thrive only if a large number of people aspire one day to run for office. For that reason, our results ultimately paint a grim picture about the prospects for an engaged citizenry and a healthy democracy. Our brightest and most able young citizens are gener-ally not open to seeking or holding positions of political power.

These findings are particularly worrisome because they have emerged despite the movement that propelled Barack Obama to the White House in 2008. The campaign, which succeeded in no small part because of young people's enthusiasm and volunteerism, seems ultimately to have failed to transform budding political interest into political ambition. According to John Della Volpe, the director of polling at Harvard's Institute of Politics, "If you were to call it an Obama generation, there was a window. That opportunity has been lost."[10] The reasons for President Obama's failure to sustain young people's political engagement are multifold, but we are reluctant to conclude that the situation is entirely hopeless. Motivating young people to aspire to run for office—especially in the current environment—is without question a daunting challenge. But it is not insurmountable.

Young Americans are committed to improving their communities and the world, which means that the potential for political leadership is in place. But the performance of government and politicians, coupled with the shallow and negative way the news media cover politics, discourages the vast majority of them from even thinking about running for office. Thus, in this final chapter, we draw from the lessons we learned about how young people feel about entering politics and consider ways we can alter their perceptions. Changing the playing field so that politics is a more appealing endeavor for young people will be difficult, but we conclude the chapter with five recommendations to steer us in the right direction.

The 11 Percent: Lessons from Politically Ambitious Young People

This book paints a bleak picture of young people's ambition to become political leaders. As we begin to think about ways to alter their mindset, though, we should keep in mind the good news. Most of the young people we surveyed and interviewed have a sincere commitment to improve their communities and the world. The majority already have many attributes that would make them good candidates and elected officials. They consider themselves leaders and have clear notions of what successful leadership entails. And they all live in a world where political connectedness and engagement have never been easier. The rise of digital media allows people to participate in politics in ways that were impossible even a mere 10 years ago.[11] Following a candidate, supporting a cause, writing a blog post, or emailing a political leader are literally at the fingertips of anyone with a digital device.

The bad news, of course, is that only 11 percent of the young people we surveyed were willing to consider running for office in the future. Taking a closer look at this small group can help us determine what differentiates them from their non-politically ambitious peers. Who are these young people? What do they have in common? What traits and backgrounds do they share? Chapters 3, 4, and 5 identify several characteristics and experiences that are linked to political ambition. But we can gain an even better sense of the influence of each of these factors by comparing the 11 percent of young people who were open to the idea of running for office with the 89 percent who were not (many of whom dismissed it after only a moment's thought).[12]

The left-hand column of Table 6.1 presents data from the 449 people—out of the more than 4,000 we surveyed—who reported that they were open to (or, for some, even enthusiastic about) the idea of running for office in the future. The right-hand column summarizes the backgrounds and experiences of the 89 percent who reported no interest in running for office. There are many differences between the two groups. More specifically, the 11 percent were more than twice as likely as the 89 percent to discuss politics with their parents regularly or to participate in any political activities with them. They were also more than three times as likely to have been encouraged to think about running for office by their parents or other family members.

Table 6.1 Comparing Young People with Political Ambition to Those without It

	The 11% (Who Would Consider Running for Office)	The 89% (Who Would Not Consider Running for Office)
Chapter 3: Family Experiences		
Talks with a parent about politics at least a few times a week	56%	24%
Has engaged in at least four political activities with a parent	28	14
Mother has encouraged a candidacy	64	20
Father has encouraged a candidacy	52	16
Other family member has encouraged a candidacy	48	14
Chapter 4: Politics at School, with Friends, and through the Media		
Took a political science or government class at school	60	44
Ran for student government	57	17
Talks about politics with friends at least weekly	51	12
Visits political websites at least weekly	71	21
Chapter 5: Attitudes toward Politicians		
Associates at least one positive trait with politicians	58	42
Inspired by at least one political figure	72	47
N	449	3,828

Notes: Entries indicate the percentage of respondents within each subsample who reported having each trait, experience, or impression. All comparisons between the 11 percent and the 89 percent are statistically significant at p < .05.

The 11 percent were one-third more likely to have taken a government course, which is remarkable given high school and college curricular requirements that often mandate such classes. And they were between three and four times as likely to immerse themselves in politics outside the classroom, whether through extracurricular activities, discussions with friends, or online. Not surprisingly, they were approximately 40 percent more likely to think positively about politicians and 50 percent more likely to be inspired by them.

Perhaps politically ambitious young people seek out political information because they are interested in campaigns, elections, and government. Or maybe political exposure has been thrust upon them because their parents, teachers, and friends happen to be political junkies. Regardless of the reason for the heightened exposure, the immersion into politics pays off when it comes to political ambition. Those who tune in are far less likely to be turned off. The key to generating more political ambition among today's young people, then, seems to be hooking them on electoral politics and maintaining their interest, despite the unappealing nature of much of what they'll see.

Charting a New Course: Five Ways to Inspire Young People to Run for Office

How can we get more young people to aspire to run for office? The simple solution is for government to function more effectively, politicians to act more responsibly, and the news media to cover politics more substantively. If young people saw politics as a vibrant, effective way to engage with and improve their communities and society, then more of them would not be turned off by the thought of entering the fray. We would be remiss, therefore, not to implore politicians and journalists to consider the consequences of their actions beyond one budget cycle, one election, or one newscast. But we are not naïve enough to believe that major changes to the performance of US government, or how the news media report on politics, are anywhere on the horizon. A snowball has a better chance in hell than does an open call to politicians to behave better.

Another fix could take place in the classroom. Civic education programs in schools are certainly generating a sense of civic responsibility, but alone—as we've shown—they don't trigger a broad interest in politics or future office-seeking. If high schools and colleges systematically integrated politics and public policy into their curricula, though, students might develop a more expansive sense of the importance of government and public affairs. Science classes could cover topics like stem cell research, medical marijuana, and global warming, and evaluate the evidence used by policymakers on both sides of each issue to make their case. Math classes could model how to balance state and federal budgets. Economics classes could assess the domestic and global consequences of raising the debt ceiling or shutting down the government. Curricular initiatives that highlight the importance of politics and the role of local and state elected officials might allow young people to see the wide-ranging relevance of politics and gain a more nuanced view of how government operates. But here, too, it is important to be realistic. Across the country, local school districts engage in regular and dramatic disputes over teaching evolution, climate change, and even basic US history.[13] Cooperation on any type of initiative that would integrate politics into curricula more broadly is, to say the least, unlikely.

Thus, in developing a series of recommendations to stimulate young people's political ambition, we think it is vital to recognize why they are currently turned off to politics, why they do not immerse themselves in it, and how we can change that. Our recommendations require motivation, commitment, and funding from entrepreneurs, educators, activists, journalists, and politicians. But, if implemented, each has the potential to change young people's attitudes toward politics and jumpstart their political ambition.

Recommendation # 1: The YouLead Initiative

In 1961, John F. Kennedy signed an executive order that established the Peace Corps. Since then, it has sent hundreds of thousands of Americans abroad "to tackle the most pressing needs of people around the world."[14] The Peace Corps' domestic counterpart AmeriCorps—places thousands of people each year in community-service-related jobs at nonprofit organizations, schools, and public agencies throughout the United States. Founded in 1994, the organization has deployed 800,000 Americans to "meet critical community needs in education, public safety, health, and the environment."[15] And for the last 25 years, Teach for America has recruited more than 30,000 recent college graduates and young professionals to "build the movement to eliminate educational inequity." Teachers commit to a two-year position at an impoverished urban or rural public school.[16] Together, these programs send a strong signal that the government values, and American society depends on, volunteer work and public service.

If we are to change the current trajectory of young people's political ambition, a good place to start would be with a similar type of national initiative—one that promotes the importance of running for office and inspires the next generation of political leaders, a program that holds politics in the same regard as other noble endeavors. We don't mean to overlook organizations like Envision, the Hugh O'Brien Youth Leadership Foundation, Youth to Leaders, the Youth Leadership Institute, or the National Youth Leadership Council, all of which focus on developing young people's leadership skills in general.[17] And Boys State and Girls State, started in the 1930s and run by the American Legion and the American Legion Auxiliary, respectively, teach young people about the responsibility of citizenship and the functioning of the government.[18] But none of these organizations focuses specifically on cultivating the next generation of elected leaders, and none has been able to achieve the kind of widespread national attention and acclaim that the Peace Corps enjoys. Accordingly, we propose the YouLead initiative, which would seek to improve the health and vitality of American democracy by urging young people to consider running for office. Whether developed as a government program or a massive nonprofit endeavor, YouLead would have three key components.

First, the initiative would strive to convince young people that running for office is a worthwhile, appealing, effective way to serve the community, country, or world. If young people don't like what's happening in their schools, then they should think about running for the school board someday. If high school or college students have an idea about how to bring more businesses or jobs to the area where they live, then they should consider a seat on the town or city council. If young Americans are upset with their state's minimum wage, then they might be well-suited to run for the state legislature. And if they think that federal taxes are too high or too low, environmental restrictions too lax or too burdensome, or government surveillance too intrusive or too limited, then Congress might be a good place to serve.

Transmitting this message is easier said than done, but a savvy national media campaign that reaches young people through digital devices and social media is a good place to start. If *Schoolhouse Rock* could use a three-minute musical cartoon to teach generations of young people how a bill becomes a law, then a fun, upbeat public service campaign about "How a Kid Becomes a Mayor" or "How a Kid Goes to Washington" could generate similar appeal.[19] Not only would these videos be educational, but they would also plant the seed very early in life that running for office is a great way to solve problems and make a difference. As we saw in our survey, about three-quarters of high school and college students today identify making the community a better place as one of their major life goals. A national campaign that links politics to community service could demonstrate that politics is about more than partisan warfare in Washington, DC.

The second critical aspect of YouLead would involve presenting the possibility of a different kind of politics. As we have hammered home throughout this book, when young people think about politics, they conjure up images of self-interested, egotistical conservatives fighting self-interested, egotistical liberals to the point of government paralysis. Only if we can change those perceptions will young people consider throwing their hats into the ring. Again, this is easier said than done. Some Washington-based organizations have been trying to change politics for quite some time. The Third Way, for example, is a center-left think tank that advances pragmatic policy solutions on a wide range of issues. They boast on their website that the media have labeled them "incorrigible pragmatists" and the "best source for new ideas in public policy."[20] Main Street Advocacy fights ideological dogma and hyperpartisanship from the other side of the political aisle. The conservative group seeks to "reach out to independents, disaffected Republicans and Democrats, centrists, suburbanites, and young voters, offering pragmatic, common sense solutions to the complex challenges facing our country today."[21] Given recent events in Washington, and Americans' utter disgust with politicians, though, these organizations have not made much headway.

YouLead would take a different tack than proposing common-ground solutions at the federal level. The program's message would be that young people themselves are needed to foster new leadership, and that we can look to lower levels of government for examples. The program could place the spotlight on local leaders—most of whom are not professional politicians, have never been tainted by scandal, and aren't prolific fundraisers or media-seeking narcissists. With a series of engaging video profiles of regular men and women who hold elected office because they care about the community and are making positive change, YouLead would seek to change young people's impressions of politicians, many of which are based on federal officeholders behaving badly.

The third component of YouLead would entail encouraging potential leaders—directly—to consider a future in politics. Regional and state coordinators for the program would identify high school and college students who have already exhibited leadership success. Student government leaders are obvious candidates, but captains of sports teams, members of debate and mock trial teams, and those participating in drama and musical performances would be excellent contenders, too. Our survey results show that early life experiences that foster competition or facilitate a public persona correlate with political ambition.

Young people who played organized sports and said that it was very important to win, for example, were four times more likely than those who did not to be interested in running for office. By identifying these young people, inviting them to a regional conference, and teaching them how to channel their leadership capabilities into electoral politics, YouLead would encourage our best and brightest to think about running for office. The program could even capitalize on their competitive spirit by hosting a national conference to which regional participants could apply.

Founding YouLead would require substantial support from educators, coaches, mentors, parents, elected officials, and donors. But if we want to put the next generation on the path to politics, then what better way to do it than by demonstrating that running for office is just as valuable and effective a form of service as is volunteering to improve conditions in communities throughout the country and across the globe?

Recommendation # 2: PlayStation for Politics

Young people play video games. A lot of video games. According to a recent Pew study of 12–17 year olds, 97 percent play these games; 50 percent of those polled played one the previous day.[22] A 2010 Kaiser Family Foundation poll of 8–18 year olds found that the typical young person plays 13.2 hours of video games each week.[23] The trend continues in college, where the average male freshman engages in more than 14 hours a week of video-game play; women average a little less than 10 hours.[24] This was true in our survey of high school and college students, too. Roughly two-thirds reported playing video games daily, and more than one in five played for at least two hours a day. Video games are clearly part of the new media frontier that is second nature to young people.

Although the most popular games fall within the action, adventure, or fantasy genres, many are a bit more educational, teaching players about capitalism, history, military strategy, urban planning, or engineering. In *Alice Greenfingers*, for instance, players learn how to start a farming business. They must think about how to price crops, promote their business, expand their farm, and use natural resources. Other games teach young people how to open and manage restaurants, hotels, bakeries, hair salons, and pet-grooming shops. And games like *SimCity* and *Minecraft* require players to build and plan entire cities. Contrary to many people's expectations, playing video games can actually boost civic and political engagement. Moderate-use video-game players are more likely than those who do not play to keep up with current events, raise money for causes, and attempt to persuade their peers about who to support in an election.[25]

If politics and running for office are to appear on young people's radar screens, why not ensure that they encounter politics in the media realms they currently inhabit? We propose a series of video games that would immerse young people in the world of politics. Imagine a game in which the player is a candidate for public office, like mayor, governor, member of Congress, or president of the United States. The object of the game would be for the candidate to get on the ballot, win the primary, and then win the general election. Along the way, players would be required to make multiple decisions: When should they file their candidacy? Which campaign staffers will they hire? How much time do they need to spend raising money? Should they air negative ads about their opponents? Should they seek endorsements and accept donations from interest groups, PACs, and political parties? Can they withstand temptations—like cheating on a spouse with a campaign volunteer or accepting a gift from a donor—that often result in scandals that can sink a campaign? Each decision a player makes would influence her electoral prospects, some for better and some for worse.

Or consider a game in which players are elected officials who must create and enact new laws. Players would choose a policy area—such as taxes, gun control, or immigration—and then steer their bill through the legislative process. Again, they would have to deal with a host of challenges: building winning coalitions, facing pressure from lobbyists, navigating a highly partisan legislature, to name only a few. And they would have to make difficult choices: Should they compromise with their political opponents and risk electoral defeat? Should they take bribes? Should they meet with corporate lobbyists? What about leaking damaging personal information about their political enemies?

Some precedent for this idea already exists. In 2003, Steven Johnson wrote an article for *slate.com* asking why no good political video games focus on US politics: "Political simulations are practically ubiquitous in the gaming world, but you're more likely to find a game that will let you stage a Spartacus-style slave revolt than one that will let you win the Iowa caucuses."[26] Since then, a host of video games about American politics have come on the market. *The Political Machine* and *Whack a Candidate*, for example, allow players to choose from existing presidential candidates and try to win the election. *Democracy 3* puts the player in the shoes of the president, who must navigate both the policy-making and electoral processes.[27] Some educators and organizations have also started using political video games as educational tools. In 2008, for instance, the Woodrow Wilson International Center for Scholars developed *Budget Hero*, which gives players the opportunity to try to balance the federal budget by implementing tax and spending increases and cuts.[28]

The Annenberg Center at the University of Southern California promotes *The Redistricting Game*, which helps people understand the system of redistricting and the consequences of partisan gerrymandering.[29]

Many of these games have been well-received as fun educational tools, mostly for college students. But few approach the real-life dramatic gaming experience most young people expect and enjoy. In many cases, the graphics are not very advanced. The challenges and obstacles players face are not very complex. And the degree of creativity required on the part of the player is often quite limited. But given the intricacies of electoral politics in the United States, more sophisticated games could certainly take hold and combat young people's disinterest from politics. Players might initially be drawn to the game because of the drama and the challenges. But they could get hooked on politics in the process.

Recommendation # 3: Political Ambition—Put That in Your Bong and Smoke It

Despite the subheading, no, we do not suggest broadening the campaign to legalize marijuana as a way to increase political ambition among young people. (Although, who knows? Given that more than half the population under the age of 25 admits to having smoked pot, it might work.[30]) We do, however, propose making political engagement a fundamental part of the college experience. Most K–12 education systems in the United States urge young people to become involved in their communities and to vote as soon as they turn 18. But these messages have seen limited success in generating political activity and ambition. Unfortunately, there is little incentive for young people to stay informed about politics. The unappealing features of the current political system only compound the problem. So, an effective way to increase young people's political interest and exposure is to appeal to their sense of self-interest. The primary educational goal of 12–17 year olds is to attend college (roughly 85 percent of the high school students we surveyed planned to go to college). Why not link political aptitude to the college application process? It would actually be pretty easy to do.

Changing the current system of college preparedness can be addressed from two angles: the structure of the college admissions process, and the social and cultural aspects of how young people learn about college life. Turning first to college admissions, we encourage colleges and universities to require applicants to demonstrate that they are on track to becoming engaged citizens who know something about current political events, both domestically and internationally. The five key ingredients in a college application—high school grades, standardized test scores, lists of extracurricular activities, personal essays, and letters of recommendation—make it entirely possible for students to apply to, and be accepted at, even the most prestigious schools without any civic interest or political knowledge.[31] You can't find Iraq on a map? That's okay. You don't know the name of the vice president of the United States? No big deal. You're unfamiliar with which political party controls Congress? Don't worry about it. This must change. We need to begin to take seriously the proposition that if young people can't answer questions like these—questions that indicate at least a modicum of familiarity with the political world and a willingness to be engaged citizens in a democratic country—then perhaps they are not ready for college.[32] Young people who are not even aware that there are major political battles being fought over the federal budget, climate change, immigration reform, or gay rights should not be welcomed into a university setting as if their lack of knowledge is not a problem.

We should be clear that in no way do we mean to suggest that some people should not be able to go to college. Quite the contrary. We want to ensure that politics and current events are important for pursuing higher education so that high school students cannot choose to be tuned out. Accordingly, we propose that some aspect of the college application process includes political awareness. This could be in the form of a new component to the SAT or other entrance exam, an additional exam that focuses on politics and citizenship, or an essay devoted to world affairs and politics. David Mindich actually advocated for the inclusion of a current-events test as part of the college admissions process in 2004, but little came of his suggestion. Over the course of the last decade, however, high school and college students have become lower performing on a wide array of measures, including political aptitude. In Oklahoma and Arizona, for example, only about 3 percent of high school students would pass a US citizenship test. The time, therefore, might be particularly ripe to revisit the idea.[33]

The vehicle is almost incidental; what matters is that the college admissions process would force young people to take news and information gathering seriously, if for no other reason than it is required for a successful college application. In fact, a similar method has generated a sense of volunteerism and community service among high school students. Roughly 75 percent of high school seniors do some sort of volunteer work.[34] One factor propelling such high levels of engagement, no doubt, is that it improves the college application. *Mycollegeguide.org*, an online guidebook sent to high-achieving high school sophomores and juniors, urges prospective college applicants to volunteer because it will "impress" college admission officers.[35]

The second aspect of college preparedness concerns the way college counselors, guidebooks, and websites characterize college life. This, too, must change. A cursory scan of some of the most popular college guidebooks—like the *Fiske Guide to Colleges* or Princeton Review's *379 Best Colleges*—includes little or no mention of the importance of political engagement as a component of college life. Even bestselling books geared toward the lived experience of college students—such as *The Naked Roommate* or *1001 Things Every College Student Needs to Know*—never mention the importance or benefits of reading a newspaper, taking a government class, or talking about world events with friends. And when prospective college students google "things to know about college" or "suggestions for new college students," they are inundated with dozens of lists and recommendations about how to study, separate from their parents, maintain their physical and mental health, and date on campus. The list goes on and on, but nowhere do they see anything about the importance of being a politically engaged citizen. College professors are impressed by students who know what's going on in the world (we can personally attest to this). But this sort of tip is nowhere to be found.

A collective effort by those involved in the college admission process to emphasize the merits of being an informed citizen would send a clear message to young people that they are expected to know something about politics. Political ambition can only emerge if young people are politically aware. Tying that awareness to the college admissions process is a relatively painless, but fruitful, way to bolster engagement. Although the habit of staying politically informed may fade once students submit their applications, it might not. As more young people acquire the habit of consuming news, they may find that their heightened exposure actually increases their interest. And there is no downside for colleges and universities to take the position that to be successful citizens, students must be connected to the world around them.

Recommendation # 4: Girl Uninterrupted—Increase College Women's Political Ambition

The overwhelming majority of young people are not interested in running for office. But, as we noted in chapter 3, a substantial gender gap in political ambition exists among college students—a gap that is not present among high school boys and girls (see Figure 6.1). College men were twice as likely as women to report that they'd definitely be interested in running for office in the future. College women, on the other hand, were almost 60 percent more likely than men to say they would never run. More specifically, 20 percent of college men, compared to 10 percent of college women, were willing to consider running for office in the future and had thought about it many times. Fourteen percent of men, but only 7 percent of women, reported that they "definitely" planned to run. On the opposite side of the political ambition continuum, 36 percent of women, compared to 23 percent of men, articulated "absolutely no interest" in a future candidacy. These gender gaps persist when we focus on specific offices. Men were three times more likely than women to be open to running for president. They were twice as interested in being a member of Congress. Although overall levels of interest in running for office are low, the gender differences among college students are substantial. In fact, the size of the gender gap in political ambition among college students is comparable to the size of the gap we previously uncovered in studies of potential candidates.

Many factors contribute to the gender gap in political ambition, as we explain in a report entitled *Girls Just Wanna Not Run*.[36] Just consider four key gender differences we identified among the college students we surveyed:

- Men were more likely than women to be encouraged by their parents to think about politics as a career.

- From school to friends to media habits, women reported less political discussion and exposure than men did.
- Women were less likely than men to receive the suggestion to run for office—from anyone.
- Women were less likely than men to think they would be qualified to run for office, even later in life after they've established their careers.

Figure 6.1 The Gender Gap in Young People's Political Ambition, by Age

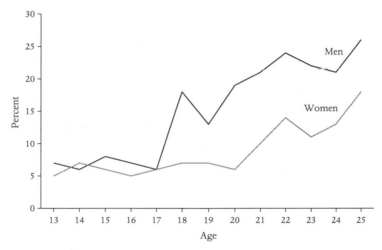

Notes: For women, N = 2,136; for men, N = 2,141. The gender gaps are not statistically significant for high school students (ages 13–17). Among college students (ages 18–25), the gender differences are statistically significant at $p < .05$ for all age groups.

Any strides aimed specifically at combatting the reasons for the gender gap in college students' political ambition would result in a marked increase in the overall proportion of young people who might be interested in running for office. Sustained parental encouragement and support for daughters to consider a future in politics, for example, would go a long way. Organizational efforts to engage young women politically during the college years are a particularly practical and efficient way to proceed. Because female college students are less likely than men to take political science classes, discuss politics with their friends, and seek out political information through the media, there are substantial opportunities for women's organizations—on college campuses and nationally—to make a difference. Thus, we propose that organizations that already exist and have a well-established infrastructure expand their reach.

Consider IGNITE, which runs political and civic-education and training programs in high schools in California and Texas. The organization identifies 15 high school girls at participating schools and offers an afterschool training program for three hours each week throughout the school year. Annually, hundreds of participants learn about government (particularly at the local level), issues they consider personally relevant (such as immigration, reproductive rights, marriage equality, and education funding), and the importance of women in politics. A central component of the IGNITE model also involves introducing high school girls to female candidates and elected officials who can share their personal stories. At the college level, though, IGNITE's programming is far more limited; the organization offers one 10-hour training session on participating campuses.[37]

Or look at Running Start. The organization "introduces young women to role models, talks to young women about the importance of politics in their lives, and gives them the encouragement and skills to pursue a career in political leadership."[38] The bulk of the programming, however, focuses on high school students. Its flagship Young Women's Leadership Program is a six-day retreat for 50 high school girls from across the country.

The weeklong foray into politics includes workshops on public speaking, networking, fundraising, media training, and issue advocacy. Young female candidates and elected officials are also integral to the program; they speak to participants about what it is like to run for office, why it matters, and how to get involved at the local level. Here, too, though, programming beyond the high school level is far less developed. The organization offers an annual day-long Young Women's Political Summit (for women under the age of 35), which touches on many of the same topics.

Programs like these are vital for ensuring that high school girls are just as politically interested as high school boys. But we need to create and develop initiatives directed at college women. After all, the gender gap in political ambition skyrockets when students set foot on college campuses. High-profile, bipartisan women's advocacy groups, such as the National Organization for Women, NARAL, and the Women's Campaign Fund, would be well served to launch national initiatives on college campuses. Partisan organizations, like Emily's List, Emerge America, or even the Democratic and Republican Parties themselves, would also benefit from developing a substantial collegiate presence. These organizations are well positioned to provide college women with continued exposure to female candidates and elected officials. Their sustained efforts would show young women how running for office can bring about societal change. And the programs would help combat women's tendency to doubt their abilities to enter politics. We asked respondents whether they thought that, after they finish college and have been working for a while, they will know enough and be sufficiently prepared to run for office. College men were more than twice as likely as women to answer the question affirmatively. College women, on the other hand, were 50 percent more likely than men to doubt that they would be qualified.[39] The organizations would win, too. By casting a wider net, all of these groups would expand their own pools of potential female candidates down the road.

We understand that raising money for programs and initiatives like these is difficult. And we recognize that it is often easier to corral high school students than college students into particular groups and activities. But our data make a compelling case for expanding the reach of organizations that are already doing excellent work bringing women into the political process. We know that once a young woman is encouraged to run for office, she is just as likely as a young man to be open to a future in politics. The challenge is to send that message to more college women. We hope that women's organizations will use our results to fundraise and convince the donor community—individuals, foundations, and corporations—that this would be money well spent.

Recommendation # 5: The GoRun App

We live in the era of the app. There are apps for everything imaginable. Looking to watch a movie on your phone or tablet? Netflix has an app for that. Want to receive an alert five minutes before it's going to rain or snow wherever you happen to be? Just download the Darksky app. Wonder what's going on in your neighborhood? The AroundMe app can tell you within seconds. You can check *Facebook*, call for an Uber, pay a bill, find cheap airline tickets, locate the closest Mexican restaurant, or listen to your favorite music with the simple touch of an app.

Digital devices and their apps serve as the modern mode of information gathering and communication for young people, most of whom are digital junkies. Roughly three-quarters of high school juniors and seniors and more than 90 percent of college students carry mobile devices with Internet access. And they use them incessantly. Consider these statistics from the *Mobile Youth Report*:

- 81% of people under the age of 25 sleep with their phone next to them on the bed.
- 74% report reaching for their smartphones as the first thing they do when they wake up.
- 97% of teens regularly use smartphones in the bathroom to check messages.[40]

There seems to be no activity, time of day, or location that is out of bounds for young people's smartphone and app use.

So, as a final suggestion, we propose taking advantage of the digital world young people inhabit by creating an app that helps them identify political offices and informs them about how to run for them. As strange as it might sound, it is actually quite difficult to find out what elected positions exist in any given community, let alone determine the nuts and bolts involved in running for them. Try asking a group of high school or college students, even those very interested in politics, the first thing someone who wants to run for office should do and they will likely give you a blank stare. There is no central clearinghouse that provides this kind of information. An interested person might try the secretary of state or board of elections website to obtain a list of positions. But in some localities, only the county or city clerk sites contain this information. In others, it's the political parties that run primary elections. Assuming that a person manages to identify the elected offices in her community, she still needs to search the site for key information, such as primary and general election dates, procedures for getting on the ballot, campaign finance rules, and the names of the incumbents who occupy each post. And virtually no website for any of the states, let alone counties or cities, notes the key responsibilities of each position. The critical pieces of information that anyone contemplating a candidacy might need are not easy to unearth.

The GoRun app would allow users to enter their address and receive a complete list of all the elected positions representing that residence—from the local school board all the way up to president of the United States. Clicking on each position would result in a definition of the office, a set of core responsibilities, and all relevant information about the logistics and rules required to run. Figuring out how to become a candidate would literally be at young people's fingertips, as would identifying the positions that best meet their interests. High school teachers and college professors could easily incorporate the app into their curricula to show students how to get involved in their communities and learn about the many electoral opportunities they could pursue. And young people who are even the least bit curious as to how to run for office would not have to engage in a fact-finding mission that can be a frustrating deterrent.

While perhaps revolutionary in its ability to make the process of running for office more accessible, creating the app would be a substantial undertaking. Given the sheer number of elected positions in the United States, building this app would require assembling and maintaining a massive database of several hundred thousand elected offices. But developing it cannot be any more logistically difficult than creating the apps and databases that monitor millions of young people's consumer preferences and suggest to them what movies they might like to watch, what songs they might like to download, or what vacations they might like to take. With interest and financing from a wealthy foundation, corporation, or philanthropist devoted to civic engagement, the challenge is certainly manageable and the potential benefits considerable. Billionaires Sheldon Adelson, Warren Buffet, and Bill Gates recently came together to scold Congress for its refusal to pass immigration reform, writing in the *New York Times* that they want to encourage "535 of America's citizens to remember what they owe to the 318 million who employ them."[41] Think about what these wealthy entrepreneurs could accomplish if they marshalled their resources to make it easier for the 318 million to step forward and engage their democracy.

When All Is Said and Done . . .

We began this book by asking why young people like Aliza, Stacy, Peter, and Terry—who have their whole lives in front of them—have already decided that they'd never run for office. Six chapters, 115 interviews, and thousands of surveys later, the answer is pretty clear. Our political system turns young people off to the idea of running for office, discourages them from aspiring to be elected leaders, and alienates them from even thinking about a career in politics. While steering a new course will be difficult, anyone who cares at all about the future of US democracy should take seriously the problems we chronicle in this book and the recommendations we outline in this chapter. Young people have the skills and potential to make the country and the world a better place. Let's make sure they see that running for office is a worthwhile way to do it.

Chapter 1

1. To protect anonymity, we changed the names and modified the identifying references of the people we surveyed and interviewed for this book. But the backgrounds we describe and the quotes we include come directly from the surveys we administered and the interviews we conducted.

2. Political scientists offer nuanced accounts of the causes and consequences of a political system mired in legislative gridlock, policy stalemates, and party polarization. Some argue that intra-branch conflict is the main culprit (Binder 1999). Others suggest that the parties' constituencies have become more politically and ideologically aligned (Richman 2011; Sinclair 2006), thereby leading members to cede more power to their party leaders, many of whom implement procedures that exacerbate polarization (Theriault 2008). And still others link polarization to the redistricting process (Carson et al. 2007), or to elected officials' obsession with instantaneous feedback—made easy in the digital age—from poorly informed constituents (Goidel 2013).

Regardless of the underlying causes, today's polarized system affects the legislative process and the public's attitudes. More specifically, a highly polarized legislative environment reduces incentives for cooperation (Gilmour 1995) and policy innovation (Barber and McCarty 2013), and makes it difficult to pass bills (Jones 2001; McCarty 2007). Moreover, because people are more likely to trust politicians who share their preferences, polarization increases distrust of government and elected officials with whom citizens disagree (Bafumi and Herron 2010; Keele 2005; Nye, Zelikow, and King 1997). Members of highly polarized parties are also more likely to engage in name-calling and ad hominem attacks (Jamieson and Falk 2000), as well as run negative ads against their opponents (Geer 2006), both of which can further alienate voters.

For recent book-length treatments of the roots and ramifications of party polarization and legislative gridlock, see Binder 2003; Lee 2009;

Theriault 2013; 2008. And for a list of some of the most shocking recent examples of the incivility exhibited on Capitol Hill, as compared to the decorum and pragmatism practiced by "old style" members of Congress, see Ahuja 2008.

3. Bill Clinton, *My Life* (New York: Knopf, 2004), page 63.

4. Gail Sheehy, "The Inner Quest of Newt Gingrich," *Vanity Fair*, September 1995. Accessed at: http://www.pbs.org/wgbh/pages/frontline/newt/vanityfair1.html (February 13, 2014).

5. Shannon Canton, "Family Business," *Delaware Today*, July 2003. Accessed at: http://www.delawaretoday.com/Delaware-Today/September-2008/The-Biden-Archive-Family-Business/(February 14, 2014).

6. A large interdisciplinary literature examines the way that early career aspirations link to professional goals and predict career trajectories. For examples of studies in this vein, see Ashby and Schoon 2010; Brown et al. 2001; Mello 2008; Schoon 2001; Schoon and Parsons 2002; Schoon and Polek 2011; Trice and McClellan 1993.

7. Negative campaigns have become the norm in high-level American politics (West 2009). And even if the substance of campaigns has not moved in a decidedly negative direction since the 1960s, negativity in conduct has become more widely publicized in the modern era (Buell and Sigelman 2008). Because the media are more likely to cover negative ads, campaigns have a greater incentive to produce them (Geer 2013; see also Lau and Rovner 2009; Ridout and Smith 2008).

   Exacerbating the negativity produced by campaigns and politicians are journalistic norms and the emergence of a partisan media. The media tend to focus on human tragedy and triumph at the expense of broader context and analysis (Bennett 2002); and they love conflict and negativity (Geer 2012; see also Cook 1998). Moreover, as trust in the mainstream media has evaporated over time, Jonathan Ladd (2012) argues that people have turned to partisan media outlets for information. But the partisan media have an even greater incentive to highlight the most negative aspects of the stories they cover, and often rely on hyperbole to do so.

8. This research tends to link distrust of government to monumental events, such as the Vietnam War and the riots and demonstrations accompanying the civil rights movement (Hetherington 2005). Less dramatic and shorter-term political and economic circumstances, however, can also fuel fluctuations in political trust (Cook and Gronke 2005), as can presidential behavior and approval ratings (Keele 2007). Regardless of the causes of fluctuating cynicism and trust, citizens are more likely to engage the political system when they trust government and view it as responsive (Conway 1991; King 1997; Piven and Cloward 1997). Cynicism, on the other hand, leads to lower levels of political and community engagement (Cohen and Dawson 1993; Hirlinger 1992; Wilson 1991).

9. In previous work, we found that the way potential candidates view the federal government and its players affects attitudes toward the political system (Fox and Lawless 2011a). In fact, heightened cynicism toward the federal government decreases political ambition to run not only for federal office, but also state or local office. Assessments of the political environment at the national level, therefore, can leave a significant imprint on an individual's attitudes toward entering all levels of the political system as a candidate (see also Gartner and Segura 2008; Maestas et al. 2008).

10. *New York Daily News*, October 1, 2013.

11. *Washington Post*, October 1, 2013.

12. *NBC Nightly News*, October 3, 2013.

13. John Cassidy, "The Biggest Threat to the U.S. Economy? Washington Dysfunction," *CNN.com*, October 31, 2013. Accessed at: http://money.cnn.com/2013/10/31/news/economy/gridlock-economy.pr.fortune/ (February 9, 2014).

14. Kerbel and Bloom 2005, page 13 (see also Baum and Groeling 2008; Borah 2014; Davis 2009; Hennessy and Martin 2006).

15. The Ronald Reagan Presidential Foundation and Library, Press Conference from August 12, 1986. Accessed at: http://www.reaganfoundation.org/reagan-quotes-detail.aspx?tx=2079 (February 14, 2014).

16. Sam Stein, "Robert Draper Book: GOP's Anti-Obama Campaign Started Night of Inauguration," *Huffington Post*, April 25, 2012. Accessed at: http://www.huffingtonpost.com/2012/04/25/robert-draper-anti-obama-campaign_n_1452899.html (February 14, 2014).

17. Ezra Klein, "The History of the Filibuster in One Graph," *Washington Post Wonkblog*, May 15, 2012. Accessed at: http://www.washingtonpost.com/blogs/wonkblog/post/the-history-of-the-filibuster-in-one-graph/2012/05/15/gIQAVHfoRU_blog.html (February 9, 2014).

18. Michael A. Memoli, "Mitch McConnell's Remarks on 2012 Draw White House Ire," *Los Angeles Times*, October 27, 2010. Accessed at: http://articles.latimes.com/2010/oct/27/news/la-pn-obama-mcconnell-20101027 (February 13, 2014).

19. The consequences of the Tea Party's emergence have been notable. In addition to energizing white, middle-class conservatives (Williamson, Skocpol, and Coggin 2011), it has also strengthened animosity toward President Obama and the Democrats' agenda (Aldrich et al. 2014). For a thorough account of the Tea Party's rise to prominence, see Abramowitz 2012; Skocpol and Williamson 2012. And for details about the legislative tactics and behavior of congressional Republicans—especially new members of the Tea Party—during Barack Obama's first term, see Draper 2012.

20. "CQ Roll Call's Vote Studies—2013 In Review," *CQ.com*, February 3, 2014. Accessed at: http://media.cq.com/votestudies/(February 14, 2014).

21. Josh Kraushaar, "The Most Divided Congress Ever, At Least until Next Year," *National Journal*, February 6, 2014. Accessed at: http://www.

nationaljournal.com/2013-vote-ratings/the-most-divided-congress-ever-at-least-until-next-year-20140206 (February 9, 2014).

22. Catalina Camia, "McCain Jokes about Low Approval for Congress," *USA Today*, October 26, 2011. Accessed at: http://content.usatoday.com/communities/onpolitics/post/2011/10/congress-approval-john-mccain-twitter-/1#. Uubm2bPTnoY (February 9, 2014).

23. The rocky rollout of the Affordable Care Act has been well-documented in the popular press. The glitches associated with the online launch have been described as the result of "negligence" and "ignorance" that are "unforgivable." See, for example, Conor Friedersdorf, "The Stunning Negligence that Doomed Obamacare's Launch," *The Atlantic*, October 28, 2013. Accessed at: http://www.theatlantic.com/politics/archive/2013/10/the-stunning-negligence-that-doomed-obamacares-launch/280909/ (March 16, 2014); and Nick Gillespie, "The Abysmal Pathetic Obamacare Rollout," *The Daily Beast*, October 17, 2013. Accessed at: http://www.thedailybeast.com/articles/2013/10/17/the-abysmal-pathetic-obamacare-rollout.html (March 16, 2014).

24. The seeming contradiction between a broadly loathed Congress and high reelection rates for individual members has received significant scholarly attention. Incumbents tend to represent ideologically friendly districts and have substantially more money than challengers. Further, because congressional elections are usually dominated by poorly informed voters and low turnout, incumbents often have to do little more than get their name on the ballot to continue to hold their seats. For a broad overview of the incumbency advantage and congressional elections, see Cox and Katz 1996; Herrnson and Curry 2011; Jacobson 2012.

25. "Young Voters Supported Obama Less, but May Have Mattered More," *Pew Research Center for the People & the Press*, November 26, 2012. Accessed at: http://www.people-press.org/2012/11/26/young-voters-supported-obama-less-but-may-have-mattered-more/ (February 9, 2014). The Obama campaign's unprecedented use of social media tools to identify and mobilize young people played a large role in his popularity (Cogburn and Espinoza-Vasquez 2011; Hendricks and Denton 2010). In some states, young voters were more likely than older voters to have been contacted at all (Keeter, Horowitz, and Tyson 2008), and the volume of contact far exceeded that reported by young voters in 2004 (Panagopoulos and Francia 2009). As a result, pollsters identified a spike in young people's agreement with the claim, "It's my duty as a citizen to always vote" (Sander and Putnam 2010).

26. "Likely Millennial Voters Up-for-Grabs in Midterm Elections, Harvard Youth Poll Finds," *Harvard University Institute of Politics*, October 29, 2014. Accessed at: http://www.iop.harvard.edu/likely-millennial-voters-grabs-upcoming-midterm-elections-harvard-youth-poll-finds (January 14, 2015).

27. Aamer Madhani and Jim Norman, "USA TODAY/Pew Poll: Obama Struggles with Millennials," *USA Today*, December 15, 2013. Accessed at: http://www.usatoday.com/story/news/politics/2013/12/15/usa-today-poll--obama-millennials/4012257/ (February 14, 2014).

28. Ariel Edwards-Levy, "Millennials Losing Faith in Obama and Obamacare, Poll Finds," *Huffington Post*, December 4, 2013. Accessed at: http://www.huffingtonpost.com/2013/12/04/millennials-obama-poll_n_4385174.html (February 14, 2014).

29. For more on the Circle Foundation, see http://www.civicyouth.org/about-circle/.

30. For more on Rock the Vote, see http://www.rockthevote.com/about/.

31. See Damon (2011) for an examination of whether young people are prepared to assume the responsibilities of citizenship.

32. See Bauerlein (2008) for a discussion of how young people use digital devices for communication about themselves, but not as a source of education and learning about the world.

33. A wide body of scholarship has examined the relationship between education and civic engagement. The research, which considers both educational attainment and specific educational initiatives, has produced mixed findings regarding how well education enhances various aspects of democratic participation. For a review of this literature, see Flanagan and Levine 2010; Galston 2007; 2001.

34. Our canvass of major studies of young people's political attitudes uncovered no existing data set that includes questions about interest in running for office as a career goal or aspiration. Three national surveys have asked young adults about their interest in running for office. A 2009 survey of students taking the Law School Admission Test, a 2003 study of 18–24-year-old college students, and a 1995 Gallup poll of teens all reveal modest levels of interest in running for office. But none of these surveys included questions that provide insight into *why* young people are or are not interested in running for office. The only study that begins to delve more deeply into political ambition among young people is a survey of junior high school, high school, college, and adult samples in one county in central New York (Elder 2004). Although an important first step, this study's generalizability is limited by geography and a small sample size (there are fewer than 90 respondents in each of the junior high and high school student subsamples).

35. In carrying out this study, we contracted with GfK Custom Research LLC (formerly *Knowledge Networks*), which relies on a probability-based online nonvolunteer access panel. Panel members are recruited using a statistically valid sampling method with a published sample frame of residential addresses that covers approximately 98 percent of US households. The sample consists of about 50,000 adult members (ages 18 and older) and includes women and men who live in cell-phone-only households. In addition

to the adult members, the sample also includes approximately 3,000 teens, ages 13 to 17, whose parents or legal guardians provided consent, as well as several thousand individuals between the ages of 18 and 25 who are enrolled in college. In our case, panel members were supplemented with a companion sample of respondents from an opt-in web panel. The same screening criteria were used for both sample sources to identify the eligible sample for the survey, as well as to calibrate the surveys from the nonprobability sample source and to correct for sampling error and self-selection bias in the nonprobability web panels. The survey, which we fielded from September 27 to October 16, 2012, was funded by the National Science Foundation (Grant No. 115405). In the summer of 2013, we interviewed on the phone a random sample of more than 100 survey respondents.

Chapter 2

1. Although many of these positions are somewhat obscure, they are important because of the responsibilities associated with them, and because politicians often move from local to state to federal office (Black 1972; Kazee 1994; Prinz 1993; Rohde 1979; Schlesinger 1966). More than three-quarters of the members of the US Congress, for instance, have previous political experience. In addition, state legislators with ambition to seek higher office are more likely to monitor constituents' opinions than are those with no interest in one day running for higher office (Maestas 2003; see also Maestas 2000). For a description of elective bodies, elective positions, and the time commitment and compensation associated with many of them, see Lawless 2012.

2. Contested races are often considered vital for a democracy to prosper. Put simply by political scientist Sue Thomas (1998, 1), a central criterion for evaluating the health of democracy in the United States is whether citizens are willing to run for public office: "A government that is democratically organized cannot be truly legitimate if all its citizens . . . do not have a potential interest in and opportunity for serving their community and nation" (see also Mansbridge 1999).

3. This presents some challenges for understanding when people begin to think about holding public office, or when they dismiss the idea altogether. First, most studies rely on surveys and interviews of actual candidates and officeholders. The problem, of course, is that all of these people are politically ambitious; they all ran for office. These studies are useful for examining what factors inspired people to run for office in the first place, seek reelection, or run for higher office. But they cannot tell us anything about people who choose not to run. For research about the candidate emergence process among candidates and elected officials, see Canon 1993; Fulton et al. 2006; Gaddie 2004; Maestas et al. 2006; Squire 1988.

To circumvent this problem, some researchers focus on "potential candidates." But there are problems in studying the origins of political ambition among this group, too. Anything they tell us depends on distant memories of early life experiences. People's recollections of past experiences, however, are often inaccurate. Scholars have uncovered systematic errors in the relationship between memory and self, such as absent-mindedness, misattribution, and bias (see, for example, Markus 1986; Schacter 1999; Schacter, Chiao, and Mitchell 2003). A politically ambitious adult, for instance, might remember a more politicized childhood or adolescence than she actually experienced if her life today involves regular political discussion, interest, and engagement. Alternatively, an adult with absolutely no interest in running for office could very well have forgotten about the political conversations he had with his parents as a teenager, or the political science courses he took in college. These experiences are now far removed from his day-to-day life and interests, so his accuracy in reporting them is questionable.

4. Jennifer E. Manning, "Membership of the 113th Congress: A Profile," *Congressional Research Service*, March 14, 2014. Accessed at: http://www.senate.gov/CRSReports/crs-publish.cfm?pid=%260BL%2BR\C%3F%0A (March 23, 2014).

5. "Legislator Demographics," *National Conference of State Legislators*. Accessed at: http://www.ncsl.org/research/about-state-legislatures/legislator-demographics.aspx (March 23, 2014).

6. The average age of the potential candidates in our three national Citizen Political Ambition Studies is 50. The same is true for the Candidate Emergence Studies conducted by Walt Stone, Sandy Maisel, and their colleagues; 56 percent of the potential candidates are older than 55.

7. Life's Little Mysteries Staff, "More than One-Third of Americans Believe Aliens have Visited Earth," *Christian Science Monitor*, June 28, 2012. Accessed at: http://www.csmonitor.com/Science/2012/0628/More-than-one-third-of-Americans-believe-aliens-have-visited-Earth (March 23, 2014).

8. "Cell Phones Key to Teens' Social Lives, 47% Can Text with Eyes Closed," *Marketing Charts*, September 23, 2008. Accessed at: http://www.marketingcharts.com/wp/online/cell-phones-key-to-teens-social-lives-47-can-text-with-eyes-closed-6126/ (March 23, 2014).

9. Our surveys of lawyers, business leaders, educators, and activists suggest that political ambition does not continue to increase substantially over the course of the life cycle. Approximately the same proportion of potential candidates under the age of 40 and over the age of 60 have considered running for office (see Lawless and Fox 2010). Panel data from potential candidates tell a similar story. We surveyed nearly 2,000 of the same people in 2001 and 2008 and found that aggregate levels of interest in running for office were similar across the two waves of the study (see Fox and Lawless 2011a). These findings suggest that, even though college students are more likely than high school students to be politically ambitious, we should not

assume that their interest in running for office will continue to grow over time. It may be that college students' interest in running for office is the same as it will be for the rest of their lives.

10. Dalia Sussman, "Poll: Kids Don't Want to Be President," *ABC News*, January 22, 2014. Accessed at: http://abcnews.go.com/US/story?id=90114&page=1#. UcHRgufVByJ (July 7, 2014).

11. "U.S. Seen as among the Greatest Nations, but Not Superior to All Others," *Pew Research Center for People and the Press*, Washington, DC, June 30, 2011. Accessed at: http://globalpublicsquare.blogs.cnn.com/2011/07/01/pew-americans-dont-see-u-s-as-greatest-nation-on-earth/ (March 23, 2014).

Chapter 3

1. David Haglund, "Reagan's Favorite Sitcom: How *Family Ties* Spawned a Conservative Hero," *Slate*, March 2, 2007. Accessed at: http://www.slate.com/articles/arts/dvdextras/2007/03/reagans_favorite_sitcom.html#page_start (March 1, 2014).

2. The series ended in 1989 with Alex landing a high-powered, lucrative job on Wall Street. We learn in a later Michael J. Fox sitcom that Alex eventually became a Republican congressman from Ohio. *Spin City*, "Goodbye Part 2," Season 4, episode 26, May 24, 2000.

3. *Leave It to Beaver*, "Wally's Election," Season 3, episode 19, February 6, 1960.

4. Bruce Feiler, "What *Modern Family* Says about Modern Families," *New York Times*, January 21, 2011. Accessed at: http://www.nytimes.com/2011/01/23/fashion/23THISLIFE.html?pagewanted=all&_r=0 (April 17, 2014).

5. *Modern Family*, "Election Day," Season 3, episode 19, April 11, 2012.

6. Although we did not conduct a systematic analysis of sitcom transcripts to determine television characters' political ambition, our review of some of the most popular sitcoms over time suggests a trend away from political content and positive portrayals of politics. The literature on the evolution of television norms and themes does not track the incidence of politically active characters on television shows. But for an overview of the evolution of the social issues television families have discussed and avoided in the last 50 years, see *The Sitcoms of Norman Lear* (Campbell 2006). For literature that examines the political implications of television portrayals of class, race, gender, and sexual identity, see Dalton and Linder 2012; Dines and Humez 2014; Dow 2001; Holbert, Shah, and Kwak 2003.

7. For the last 50 years, scholars have identified a series of key agents that affect political attitudes and behavior. Chief among them are family, education, peer associations, and media (for a review, see Jennings 2007; Sapiro 2004; Stoker and Bass 2011). This chapter focuses on family. We address the other socializing agents in chapter 4.

8. A large literature finds, for example, that people tend to develop political attitudes and vote retrospectively. That is, they assess whether they are better off now and whether the country is better off now than it was the last time they voted. Most of this work focuses on assessments of the economy (e.g., Fiorina 1981; Holbrook, Clouse, and Weinschenk 2012; Woon 2012). But how the incumbent party handles random events, such as natural disasters, can affect retrospective evaluations, too (Healy and Malhotra 2010). Political scientists have also found that marital transitions can affect political attitudes and participation (e.g., Stoker and Jennings 1995), as can people's direct experiences with government (e.g., Erikson and Stoker 2011; Soss 1999).

9. Alva Myrdal (1941) was among the first to urge social scientists to consider the role of family when explaining individual-level behavior. The family unit as a tool of analysis in American political science scholarship has since been employed as a mechanism for understanding political socialization (Almond and Verba 1963; Beck and Jennings 1982; Hess et al. 2006; Jennings and Markus 1984; Jennings and Niemi 1981; Niemi and Hepburn 1995; Owen and Dennis 1988) and political participation and issue preferences (Burns, Schlozman, and Verba 2001; Niemi 1974; Renshon 1974). More recently, scholars have also begun to explore whether political attitudes and behaviors result not only from socialization, but also from genetics (Alford, Funk, and Hibbing 2008; 2005; Charney and English 2012; Fowler, Baker, and Dawes 2008). For some recent literature about family as a socializing agent, see Andolina et al. 2003; Jennings 2007; 2002; Jennings and Stoker 2012; Jennings, Stoker, and Bowers 2009; McIntosh, Hart, and Youniss 2007; Sapiro 2004; Verba, Schlozman, and Burns 2005. For more classic studies, see Fiorina 1981; Jennings and Markus 1984; Jennings and Niemi 1968.

10. These quotes were taken from our 2010 book, *It Still Takes a Candidate: Why Women Don't Run for Office*, which explores the gender gap in potential candidates' political ambition, and *Becoming a Candidate: Political Ambition and the Decision to Run for Office* (Lawless 2012). For additional anecdotes about the power of a politicized upbringing, see Lawless and Fox 2010, chapter 4, and Lawless 2012, chapter 5.

11. Researchers consider mealtime togetherness a barometer for the well-being of the American family. Ninety percent of parents report that mealtime is when they talk to their children about their day as well as other important topics. And studies show that, still today, most families eat dinner together most nights of the week; roughly one-third eat together all seven nights. See Ned Smith, "Family Mealtime: Most Families Eat Dinner Together Most Nights," *Huffington Post*, January 23, 2013. Accessed at: http://www.huffingtonpost.com/2013/01/23/family-mealtime-study-_n_2534347.html (July 9, 2014).

12. More specifically, 30 percent of high school seniors in 1973 reported speaking to their parents about politics and current events several times a week. Another 40% said that they had political discussions with their parents at least a few times a month. These data are from the 1973 High School Seniors Cohort Study and are based on 16,929 students from 85 schools across the country. See M. Kent Jennings, "High School Seniors Cohort Study, 1965 and 1973." ICPSR07575-vi. Ann Arbor, MI: Inter-university Consortium for Political and Social Research [distributor], 1979. Accessed at: http://doi.org/10.3886/ICPSR07575.vi (July 9, 2014).

13. Yvette M. Alex-Assensoh. 2005. *Democracy at Risk: How Political Choices Undermine Citizen Participation and What We Can Do about It.* Washington, DC: Brookings Institution Press, page 1.

14. This increases to 2.5 percent if we restrict the analysis to two-parent homes.

15. Because of differences in question wording, as well as the fact that we asked young people for their perceptions of their parents' views, we cannot compare our results to national polls that ask parents what professions they would like their children to pursue. It is important to note, though, that since Gallup asked for the first time in 1944 whether Americans would "want their sons to go into politics as a life's work" (they began asking about daughters in 1991), support for a political career has never been particularly high. In the 1940s, 19 percent of parents preferred a political career for their sons. Levels of support have ebbed and flowed since then, reaching a high of 36 percent in the mid-1960s. But generally, other professions have always been more appealing to parents. See Jeffrey M. Jones, "In U.S., 64% Want Their Child to Avoid Career in Politics," *Gallup*, July 5, 2013. Accessed at: http://www.gallup.com/poll/163373/child-avoid-career-politics.aspx (July 9, 2014); see also Karlyn Bowman, "Do You Want to Be President?" *The Public Perspective*, February/March 1997, pages 39–41.

16. *Gallup*, "Honesty / Ethics in Professions: Historical Trends." Accessed at: http://www.gallup.com/poll/1654/honesty-ethics-professions.aspx#4 (July 9, 2014).

17. These were by far the leading role models in young people's lives. To put these numbers in perspective, all other relatives—combined—served as sources of career inspiration for only 28 percent of the people who completed the survey.

18. These findings reflect patterns of socialization that promote men's greater suitability to enter the political sphere. For a discussion of how gender socialization affects political ambition, see Lawless and Fox 2010. Chapter 4, in particular, provides a detailed account of gender differences in potential candidates' family upbringings.

19. Jeffrey M. Jones, "Atheists, Muslims See Most Bias as Presidential Candidates," *Gallup*, June 21, 2012. Accessed at: http://www.gallup.com/poll/155285/Atheists-Muslims-Bias-Presidential-Candidates.aspx (April 21, 2014).

20. Abby D. Phillip and Michael Falcone, "Barbara Bush's Surprising Take on a Jeb Presidential Run," *ABC News*, January 16, 2014. Accessed at: http://abcnews.go.com/blogs/politics/2014/01/barbara-bush-really-really-doesnt-want-jeb-to-run-in-2016/ (April 21, 2014).

21. "Mrs. Romney on Sons Running for Office: Don't Do It," *The Lead with Jake Tapper*, June 6, 2013. Accessed at: http://thelead.blogs.cnn.com/2013/06/06/mrs-romney-on-sons-running-for-office-dont-do-it/ (April 21, 2014).

Chapter 4

1. See http://www.collegeprep101.com/.

2. See "A Day in the Life of a College Student." Accessed at: http://www.collegeprep101.com/a-day-in-the-life.html (April 27, 2014).

3. "Time Use on an Average Weekday for Full-Time University and College Students," *American Time Use Survey*, Bureau of Labor Statistics, 2012. Accessed at: http://www.bls.gov/tus/charts/chart6.pdf (April 30, 2014).

4. Aaron Smith, "How Americans Use Text Messaging," *Pew Research Internet Project*, September 19, 2011. Accessed at: http://www.pewresearch.org/daily-number/texting-is-nearly-universal-among young adult-cell-phone-owners/ (April 30, 2014).

5. See John H. Pryor, Kevin Eagan, Laura Palucki Blake, Sylvia Hurtado, Jennifer Berdan, and Matthew H. Case, "The American Freshman: National Norms Fall 2012," *Higher Education Research Institute, University of California, Los Angeles*. Accessed at: http://www.heri.ucla.edu/monographs/theamericanfreshman2012.pdf (April 30, 2014).

6. Mary Dorinda Allard, "How High School Students Use Time: A Visual Essay," *Monthly Labor Review*, November 2008, pages 51–61.

7. Cell phone ownership is through the roof for young people. Approximately 75 percent of 12–17 year-olds, and 97 percent of 18–29 year-olds, own a cell phone. Nearly all of those who own a mobile device report using it regularly to access social networking sites. See Amanda Lenhart, "Teens, Smartphones & Texting," *Pew Research Center*, March 19, 2012. Accessed at: http://www.pewinternet.org/files/old-media/Files/Reports/2012/PIP_Teens_Smartphones_and_Texting.pdf (April 30, 2014).

8. For a review of research on the relationship between politicized classrooms and students' political participation and efficacy, see Billig, Root, and Jesse 2005; Campbell 2008; Pasek et al. 2008.

9. Sunshine Hillygus (2005) provides a review of the research on how college life facilitates the development of politically relevant civic skills, which can then spur political interest and activism. Higher education not only provides factual knowledge about how the political system works, which can then make people feel better equipped to participate, but it can also help citizens understand that preserving a democratic system is contingent on

their political action (see, e.g., Galston 2001; Niemi and Junn 1998; Torney-Purta, Schwille, and Amadeo 1999).

10. A large body of literature focuses on civic engagement outside the classroom and how early political experiences can generate interest in politics. See, for example, Glanville 1999; Hart et al. 2007; Kirlin 2003; McFarland and Thomas 2006; Verba, Schlozman, and Brady 1995.

11. Political scientists have long identified powerful social network effects. Politically active people are more likely to be mobilized by campaigns, party leaders, elected officials, and political activists; and individuals at the center of social networks are particularly likely to be targeted (see Rosenstone and Hansen 1993; Verba, Schlozman, and Brady 1995). For recent evidence of the influence of social networks on adults' political behavior and attitudes, see Ahn, Huckfeldt, and Ryan 2010; Huckfeldt and Mendez 2008; Ryan 2011.

12. The Internet, social media, texting, and mobile devices play a major role in young citizens' daily lives. But research on whether digital devices and Internet applications encourage civic engagement in young people is mixed. In fact, a philosophical debate exists regarding what even constitutes civic engagement on a digital platform. For a series of essays examining how digital technology is changing and encouraging civic engagement in young people, see Bennett 2007 (see also Banaji and Buckingham 2010; Iyengar and Jackman 2004; Montgomery, Gottlieb-Robles, and Larson 2004). For a discussion of how young people engage new media, the extent to which they use it for participatory politics, and how it can facilitate the equitable distribution of participation across racial and ethnic groups, see Cohen et al. 2012.

13. Although we frame the analysis through an ordinary day in the life of a high school student, we are careful to call attention to relevant differences between high school and college students.

14. "Civics Education Testing Only Required in Nine States for High School Graduation: CIRCLE Study," *Huffington Post*, October 12, 2012. Accessed at: http://www.huffingtonpost.com/2012/10/12/circle-study-finds-most-s_n_1959522.html (March 12, 2014).

15. As for other mentors, 11 percent of young people identified a coach and 10 percent identified a member of the clergy as people who have inspired them or helped them think about what they might want to do in life. These mentors also offer little encouragement for a future in politics. Four percent of the young people we surveyed reported that a coach suggested that they run for office, and 5 percent received the suggestion from a member of the clergy.

16. "How Can We Encourage Youth to Participate in Democracy?" Conference on Civics Education: Why It Matters to Democracy, Society, and You, MIT Center for Civic Media, Cambridge, MA, April 1, 2013. Accessed at: http://civic.mit.edu/blog/erhardt/how-can-we-encourage-youth-to-participate-in-democracy (May 7, 2014).

17. See John H. Pryor, Sylvia Hurtado, Linda DeAngelo, Jessica Sharkness, Laura C. Romero, William S. Korn, and Serge Tran. 2008. *The American Freshman: National Norms for Fall 2008*. Los Angeles: Higher Education Research Institute, University of California, Los Angeles.

18. In 1973, only 15 percent of high school seniors reported never talking about current events with their friends. See M. Kent Jennings, "High School Seniors Cohort Study, 1965 and 1973." ICPSR07575-vi. Ann Arbor, MI: Inter-university Consortium for Political and Social Research [distributor], 1979. Accessed at: http://doi.org/10.3886/ICPSR07575.vi (July 9, 2014).

19. Rebecca J. Rosen, "59% of Young People Say the Internet Is Shaping Who They Are," *The Atlantic*, June 27, 2012. Accessed at: http://www.theatlantic.com/technology/archive/2012/06/59-of-young-people-say-the-internet-is-shaping-who-they-are/259022/ (May 4, 2014).

20. In fact, only one of the 15 most popular blogs for college students includes political content: *Huffington Post College*. See UWire, "The 20 Most Popular College Blogs." Accessed at http://uwire.com/2013/06/03/the-top-20-most-popular-college-blogs/ (May 4, 2014).

21. These results are consistent with Prior's (2007) argument about our modern "high-choice" news environment, which is characterized by access to an expanded array of media choices. People interested in politics will consume large amounts of political news. With nonstop access to national political coverage on cable television and the Internet, political junkies can indulge their interest in ways never before possible. At the same time, the less politically interested can more easily avoid political information altogether, spending their free time not with the news, but with entertainment or sports programs or websites. As a consequence, the contemporary media environment contributes to inequality in political knowledge and participation (Prior 2005). The information-rich get richer, and the information-poor get poorer.

22. Andrew Kohut, "In Changing News Landscape, Even Television is Vulnerable." *Pew Research Center for People and the Press*, September 27, 2012. Accessed at: http://www.people-press.org/files/legacy-pdf/2012%20News%20Consumption%20Report.pdf (July 10, 2014).

23. Rega Jha, "18 Apps Every College Student Should Download Right Now," *Buzzfeed*, August 8, 2013. Accessed at: http://www.buzzfeed.com/regajha/apps-every-college-student-should-download-right-now (May 4, 2014).

24. Sarah Ang, "List of 25 Apps You'll Need to Survive College," *Mashable.com*, August 8, 2013. Accessed at: http://mashable.com/2013/08/08/apps-for-college/ (May 4, 2014).

25. "Ten Must Have Apps for Successful High School Students," *Mashable.com*, August 27, 2012. Accessed at: http://mashable.com/2012/08/27/apps-for-high-school-students/ (May 4, 2014).

26. Patterson 2013, page 1. For more on the state of contemporary journalism, see Aamidor, Kuypers, and Wiesinger 2013; Anderson, Williams, and Ogola 2013; Brock 2013; McNair 2000.

27. "The Top-10 U.S. News Stories," *Time*, December 4, 2013. Accessed at: http://nation.time.com/2013/12/04/top-10-best-u-s-news-stories/ (May 5, 2014).

28. See Elizabeth Titus, "CNN Dissects Top 10 Political Stories of 2013," *Politico*, December 29, 2013. Accessed at: http://www.politico.com/blogs/politico-live/2013/12/cnn-dissects-top-political-stories-of-180305.html (May 5, 2014); and Mark Murray, "The 10 Biggest Political Stories of 2013," *NBC News*, December 18, 2013. Accessed at: http://www.nbcnews.com/politics/first-read/10-biggest-political-stories-2013-v21954175 (May 5, 2014).

29. See Andy Kohut, "Pew Surveys of Audience Habits Suggest Perilous Future for News," *Poynter*, October 7, 2013. Accessed at: http://www.poynter.org/latest-news/top-stories/225139/pew-surveys-of-audience-habits-suggest-perilous-future-for-news/ (July 10, 2014).

30. We need to be cautious when discussing the causal direction of the relationship between young people's political experiences and their political ambition. Do politically ambitious young people gravitate toward politics at school, with their friends, and in the media, or do these political activities and experiences foster their ambition in the first place? As is the case with a large body of research on political socialization, the directionality of the relationships between and among individuals' political attitudes, behaviors, and socializing factors are difficult to determine (see Fox and Lawless 2014b). The same logic (and endogeneity problem) applies when linking media exposure to increased levels of political knowledge and participation (e.g., Barabas and Jerit 2009; Delli Carpini and Keeter 1996; Jerit, Barabas, and Bolsen 2006; Larcinese 2007; Leighley 1991; Nicholson 2003). But our interviews suggest that, in many cases, classroom experiences, politicized extracurricular activities, political discussions with friends and peers, and exposure to political media can trigger interest in running for office. And even if the causal direction is tenuous, at the very least, these experiences invigorate and reinforce any ambitious tendencies students might already have.

31. Jamal Watson, "Donna Brazile Looks to Inspire Women to Enter Politics, Effect Change," *Diverse*, April 28, 2014. Accessed at: http://diverseeducation.com/article/63513/ (May 7, 2014).

32. Kim Lyons, "Donna Brazile: Women Need to Make More Progress in Legal Profession," *Pittsburgh Post-Gazette*, March 11, 2014. Accessed at: http://www.post-gazette.com/business/2014/03/12/Brazile-Women-need-to-make-more-progress-in-legal-profession/stories/201403120002 (May 7, 2014).

33. Watson, "Donna Brazile Looks to Inspire Women to Enter Politics, Effect Change."

Chapter 5

1. "John Edwards' ABC Nightline Interview, Part I," August 8, 2008. Accessed at: https://www.youtube.com/watch?v=tCc7x4z5200 (May 14, 2014).

2. "Senator John Edwards Caught with Mistress and Love Child," *National Enquirer*, July 22, 2008. Accessed at: http://www.nationalenquirer.com/celebrity/sen-john-edwards-caught-mistress-and-love-child (May 14, 2014).

3. Lee Ferran, Brian Ross, Nadine Shubailat, and Chris Francescani, "John Edwards Admits He Fathered Rielle Hunter's Child," *Good Morning America*, January 21, 2010. Accessed at: http://abcnews.go.com/GMA/john-edwards-admits-fathered-rielle-hunter-child-affair/story?id=9620812 (May 14, 2014).

4. Russell Goldman and James Hill, "John Edwards Won't Be Retried on Campaign Finance Charges," *ABC News*, June 13, 2011. Accessed at: http://abcnews.go.com/Politics/john-edwards-retried-campaign-finance-charges/story?id=16561020 (May 14, 2014).

5. Danny Hakim and William K. Rashbaum, "Spitzer Is Linked to Prostitution Ring," *New York Times*, March 10, 2008. Accessed at: http://www.nytimes.com/2008/03/10/nyregion/10cnd-spitzer.html?pagewanted=all&_r=0 (May 14, 2014).

6. Mark Jacobson, "Huma? Hey, Honey? Was I Happy before I Started Running for Mayor?" *New York Magazine*, July 14, 2013. Accessed at: http://nymag.com/news/features/anthony-weiner-2013-7/ (May 14, 2014).

7. Brian Montopoli, "GOP Congressman Christopher Lee Resigns over Craigslist Scandal," *CBS News*, February 9, 2011. Accessed at: http://www.cbsnews.com/news/gop-congressman-christopher-lee-resigns-over-craigslist-scandal/ (May 14, 2014).

8. Joel Roberts, "Senator Caught in DC Madam Scandal," *CBS News*, July 9, 2007. Accessed at: http://www.cbsnews.com/news/senator-caught-in-dc-madam-scandal/ (May 14, 2014).

9. John O'Connor and Clif LeBlanc, "Sanford Back Wednesday, His Office Says," *The State*, June 23, 2009. Accessed at: http://www.thestate.com/2009/06/23/836552/previous-coverage-sanford-back.html (May 14, 2014).

10. Kim Severson, "Looking Past Sex Scandal, South Carolina Returns Ex-Governor to Congress," *New York Times*, May 7, 2013. Accessed at: http://www.nytimes.com/2013/05/08/us/south-carolina-election-a-referendum-on-sanford.html (May 14, 2014).

11. For recent discussions of the circumstances and contexts that best allow political leaders to weather scandals, see Basinger 2014; Grover and Hasel 2014; Nyhan 2014; Rottinghaus 2014. And for an accessible summary of the research on how political scandals have affected electoral outcomes over time, see Danny Hayes, "Mark Sanford is No Exception: Most Politicians Survive Scandals," *Washington Post Wonkblog*, April 7, 2013. Accessed at: http://www.washingtonpost.com/blogs/wonkblog/wp/2013/04/07/mark-sanford-is-no-exception-most-politicians-survive-scandals/ (July 6, 2014).

12. Jim Rutenberg, "Mark Sanford's Breakup Post Caught His Fiancee Off-Guard,"*New York Times*, September 13, 2014. Accessed at: http://www.nytimes.com/2014/09/14/us/mark-sanford-mistress-affair-engagement.html?_r=0 (December 17, 2014).

13. Elise Foley, "Steve King Challenges Chuck Schumer to a Duel," *Huffington Post*, May 22, 2014. Accessed at: http://www.huffingtonpost.com/2014/05/22/steve-king-chuck-schumer_n_5374641.html?utm_hp_ref=politics (May 25, 2014).

14. Aaron Blake, "Reid: Koch Brothers are Un-American," *Washington Post*, February 27, 2014. Accessed at: http://www.washingtonpost.com/blogs/post-politics/wp/2014/02/27/reid-koch-brothers-are-un-american/ (May 27, 2014).

15. Manu Raju, "Some GOP Colleagues Angry with Ted Cruz," *Politico*, October 2, 2013. Accessed at: http://www.politico.com/story/2013/10/ted-cruz-blasted-by-angry-gop-colleagues-government-shutdown-97753.html (May 14, 2014).

16. Schuyler Kropf, "Charleston County Republicans Censure U.S. Sen. Lindsey Graham," *The Post and Courier*, May 12, 2014. Accessed at: http://www.postandcourier.com/article/20140512/PC1603/140519817/1177/charleston-county-republicans-censure-us-sen-lindsey-graham (May 14, 2014).

17. American Conservative Union, "2013 Ratings of Congress." Accessed at: http://www.conservative.org/legislative-ratings/2013-congress (December 17, 2014).

18. Ashley Killough, "Arizona GOP Rebukes McCain for Not Being Conservative Enough," *CNN.com*, January 26, 2014. Accessed at: http://politicalticker.blogs.cnn.com/2014/01/26/arizona-gop-rebukes-mccain-for-not-being-conservative-enough/comment-page-1/ (May 14, 2014).

19. Blake Neff and Molly K. Hooper, "Tea Party: Boehner Declared War," *The Hill*, December 13, 2013. Accessed at: http://thehill.com/blogs/blog-briefing-room/news/193081-tea-party-boehner-has-declared-war (May 14, 2014).

20. Samuel Bell, "In Budget Vote, Cicilline Betrays Progressives," *Rhode Island Future*, March 21, 2013. Accessed at: http://www.rifuture.org/cicilline-betrays-progressive-caucus-in-budget-vote.html (May 14, 2014).

21. "Ten Years of Progress. And Yes, We've Made Progress," *Daily Kos*, March 18, 2014. Accessed at: http://www.dailykos.com/story/2014/03/18/1285726/-10-years-of-political-progress-And-yes-we-ve-made-progress# (May 14, 2014); and Matt Bennett and Jim Kessler, "Kos Folds Up the Big Tent," *Politico Magazine*, March 19, 2014. Accessed at: http://www.politico.com/magazine/story/2014/03/daily-kos-democrats-moderates-104817.html#.U3QHfyhgF-_ (May 14, 2014).

22. Political scientists have identified a relationship between politicians' bad behavior and voters' assessments of those candidates. Scandals, for example, have been shown to reduce House incumbents' electoral margins (Abramowitz

1991; 1988) and lower citizens' evaluations of them (Clarke et al. 1999; Cowley 2002; Funk 1996; Hetherington 1999; Markus 1982; Rahn et al. 1990). But political scandals can also erode voters' trust in government and political institutions more broadly (Bowler and Karp 2004). And once a scandal increases citizens' distrust and cynicism, those negative attitudes further shape how voters process information about politicians' malfeasance (Dancey 2012).

23. For an overview of the leaders Americans most admire, see Karlyn Bowman, "Do You Want to Be President?" *The Public Perspective*, February/ March 1997, pages 39–41; Frank Newport, David W. Moore, and Lydia Saad, "Most Admired Men and Women: 1948–1998," *Gallup News Service*, December 13, 1999. Accessed at: http://www.gallup.com/poll/3415/most-admired-men-women-19481998.aspx (July 11, 2014); and "Most Admired Man and Woman," *Gallup*. Accessed at: http://www.gallup.com/poll/1678/most-admired-man-woman.aspx (July 11, 2014). When interpreting these data, keep in mind that presidential support tends to decrease over the course of a term, and that external shocks, such as 9/11, can inflate levels of admiration in the short term. The key finding is that relatively fewer Americans now most admire the president than did in previous decades.

24. Ronald E. Riggio, "Leadership 101: Who are our most admired leaders?" *Psychology Today*, January 22, 2010. Accessed at: http://www.psychologytoday.com/blog/cutting-edge-leadership/201001/leadership-101-who-are-our-most-admired-leaders (May 14, 2014).

25. Alan Fram and Trevor Tompson, "Poll: Young People's Heroes Are Parents," *USA Today*, August 20, 2007. Accessed at: http://usatoday30.usatoday.com/news/topstories/2007-08-19-2800778131_x.htm (May 17, 2014).

26. "Teen Role Models: Who They Are and Why They Matter," *Barna Group*, January 31, 2011. Accessed at: https://www.barna.org/teens-next-gen-articles/467-teen-role-models (May 17, 2014).

27. "Millennials Reveal Who Represents Their Generation," *YPulse*, November 15, 2012. Accessed at: http://www.ypulse.com/post/view/millennials-reveal-their-role-models (May 17, 2014).

28. See "Survey of Young Americans' Attitudes toward Politics and Public Service: 25th Edition," *Harvard Public Opinion Project*, April 29, 2014. Accessed at: http://www.iop.harvard.edu/sites/default/files_new/Harvard_ExecSummarySpring2014.pdf (May 16, 2014).

29. See M. Kent Jennings, "High School Seniors Cohort Study, 1965 and 1973." ICPSR07575-v1. Ann Arbor, MI: Inter-university Consortium for Political and Social Research [distributor], 1979. Accessed at: http://doi.org/10.3886/ICPSR07575.v1 (July 9, 2014).

30. More specifically, in the 1973 cohort of the "High School Seniors Cohort Study," 36 percent disagreed somewhat or strongly with the statement that public officials don't care about the people they represent. See M. Kent Jennings, "High School Seniors Cohort Study, 1965 and 1973." ICPSR07575-v1.

Ann Arbor, MI: Inter-university Consortium for Political and Social Research [distributor], 1979. Accessed at: http://doi.org/10.3886/ICPSR07575.v1 (July 9, 2014).

31. For a detailed analysis of the qualities Americans want in their political leaders, see John Hibbing and Elizabeth Theiss-Morse's (2002) *Stealth Democracy*, which argues that most people do not care very much about specific public policies and are actually quite happy to delegate decision-making authority to political leaders. It's important, however, that those decision-makers be empathetic and non-self-interested. In fact, these qualities are more important to the average citizen than whether political leaders are responsive to or in sync with their constituents' views.

32. Many scholars have developed leadership typologies that assess leadership styles contingent on situational contexts and individuals' behaviors and attitudes, among other dimensions. For reviews of the different criteria used to examine and categorize leaders, see Bass and Bass 2008; Dubrin 2012; Northouse 2012.

33. For data about the traits that voters and the media tend to consider most relevant when assessing candidates, see Hayes 2011; Hayes and Lawless 2015; Kinder 1986; Schneider and Bos 2012.

34. Scholars have long debated the fundamental question of whether leaders are born or made. For the first half of the 20th century, most examinations of leaders and leadership followed the trait approach, which is predicated on the notion that certain innate characteristics are responsible for great leadership (Stogdill 1974). But scholars began to challenge this approach, arguing that leadership qualities are often driven by situational factors. The modern study of leadership has evolved to the point that most scholars acknowledge that both character traits and situational factors influence leaders' emergence. For reviews of the literature on leadership, see Cronin and Genovese 2012; Kirkpatrick and Locke 1991; Lord, Devader, and Alliger 1986. And for a series of essays that address leadership development and success among both young people and adults, see Conger and Riggio 2007.

35. Young people who see in themselves the leadership traits that could be most useful in politics are somewhat more politically ambitious than those who do not. More specifically, 8 percent of young people who did not consider themselves confident, 9 percent of those who did not consider themselves competitive, and 9 percent of those who did not view themselves as ambitious indicated interest in running for office in the future. The main point, however, is that political ambition is quite rare, regardless of how motivated and skilled at leadership today's young people appear to be.

36. P.B.S. Pinchback was the first African American governor; he was appointed governor of Louisiana during Reconstruction and served for less than six weeks (from December 9, 1872 until January 13, 1873).

37. These data are compiled by the National Governors Association and are available on its website: http://www.nga.org/.

38. These data are provided by the black and Latino caucuses of the state legislatures and are available on the National Conference of State Legislators website: www.ncsl.org.

39. For research that uncovers a relationship between electing more black and Latino legislators and greater substantive representation of black and Latino constituents, see Canon 1999; Gamble 2007; Griffin and Newman 2007; Grose 2005; Minta 2009; Preuhs 2006.

40. More specifically, 16 percent of black respondents and 10 percent of Latinos, compared to 7 percent of white respondents, scored a three or four on the positive traits index. As far as negative assessments are concerned, 61 percent of whites, compared to 48 percent of blacks and 51 percent of Latinos, associated none of the positive traits with politicians.

41. See "Trust in Government in Washington Remains Low," *Pew Research Center*, February 12, 2013. Accessed at: http://www.pewresearch.org/daily-number/trust-in-government-in-washington-remains-low/ (July 11, 2014).

42. Brandon Griggs, "I Taught My Parents How to Text," *CNN.com*, March 12, 2014. Accessed at http://www.cnn.com/2014/03/11/tech/innovation/chelsea-clinton-sxsw/ (May 23, 2014).

43. Peter Baker and John F. Harris, "Clinton Admits to Lewinsky Relationship; Challenges Starr to End Personal 'Prying,'" *Washington Post*, August 18, 1998. Accessed at: http://www.washingtonpost.com/wp-srv/politics/special/clinton/stories/clinton081898.htm (May 26, 2014).

44. Emily Smith, "Karl Rove: Hillary Clinton May Have Brain Damage," *New York Post*, May 12, 2014. Accessed at: http://pagesix.com/2014/05/12/karl-rove-hillary-clinton-may-have-brain-damage/ (May 25, 2014).

45. Katie Glueck, "Rove: Clinton May Have Brain Injury," *Politico*, May 12, 2014. Accessed at: http://www.politico.com/story/2014/05/karl-rove-hillary-clinton-brain-injury-106613.html (May 25, 2014).

46. N.R. Keinfield, "A Bridge to Scandal: Behind the Fort Lee Ruse," *New York Times*, January 12, 2014. Accessed at: http://www.nytimes.com/2014/01/13/nyregion/a-bridge-to-scandal-behind-the-fort-lee-ruse.html?_r=0 (May 25, 2014). For an expose of the "Bridgegate" scandal, see Bryan Burrough, "Christieworld," *Vanity Fair*, August 2014.

47. Michael Barbara and Kate Zernike, "Mayor of Hoboken Says Hurricane Relief Was Threatened," *New York Times*, January 18, 2014. Accessed at: http://www.nytimes.com/2014/01/19/nyregion/florida-trip-is-no-reprieve-for-new-jersey-governor.html (May 25, 2014).

48. See Larson 2007 for a detailed discussion of the election of 1800 between Thomas Jefferson and John Adams.

Chapter 6

1. "Senator Barbara Boxer on Young People's Issues." Accessed at: https://www.youtube.com/watch?v=ZizPTihBUjE&list=PL5F6DDBBBEAF668D6 (June 16, 2014).
2. "Congresswoman Debbie Wasserman-Schultz Encourages Young People to Run for Office," Campus Progress National Conference, 2012. Accessed at: https://www.youtube.com/watch?v=wFBhBJ9R49M (June 16, 2014).
3. Danica Davidson, "29-Year-Old Congressman-Elect Patrick Murphy on Young People + Politics," *MTV.com*, December 7, 2012. Accessed at: http://act.mtv.com/posts/patrick-murphy-young-people-politics/ (June 16, 2014).
4. James Madison, "The Federalist No. 62: The Senate," *Independent Journal*, February 27, 1788.
5. See Jonathan Elliot, ed. 1836. *The Debates on the Adoption of the Federal Constitution*. Philadelphia: J. P. Lippincott, page 485.
6. Thomas Paine, "Of Monarchy and Hereditary Succession," *Common Sense*, 1776. Philadelphia: W. and T. Bradford.
7. John F. Kennedy, "Inaugural Address," January 20, 1961. Accessed at: http://www.ushistory.org/documents/ask-not.htm (June 18, 2014).
8. Jason Horowitz, "Obama Effect Inspiring Few to Seek Office," *New York Times*, April 13, 2014. Accessed at: http://www.nytimes.com/2014/04/14/us/obama-effect-inspiring-few-to-seek-office.html?partner=rss&emc=rss&smid=tw-nytimes&_r=1 (June 16, 2014).
9. Robert T. Garrett, "Senate Candidate Ted Cruz Aims to Pick Up Mantle of Reagan," *Dallas Morning News*, April 28, 2012. Accessed at: http://www.dallasnews.com/news/politics/headlines/20120428-senate-candidate-ted-cruz-aims-to-pick-up-mantle-of-reagan.ece (June 19, 2014).
10. Horowitz, "Obama Effect Inspiring Few to Seek Office."
11. A growing body of research demonstrates the ways social media and mobile devices have dramatically expanded opportunities for political engagement. Most of these analyses focus on the rise of movements and the wildfire-like diffusion of political messages, such as "We are the 99%." For reviews of how digital media are changing political participation, see Bennett and Segerberg 2014; Castells 2012; Gerbaudo 2012; Shirky 2009.
12. Certainly, political ambition exists on a continuum. Some people definitely plan to run for office and are gung ho about the idea. Others recoil at the notion and find nothing more unappealing. For most people, though, interest in entering the political arena falls somewhere between these two endpoints of the spectrum. As we documented in chapter 2, dichotomizing the continuum into two categories—those who are open to the idea of running for office at some point down the road, and those who are not—is a useful way to present and summarize the results. But these two categories are just rough approximations of ambition.

13. Curricular disputes about politics abound throughout the United States. Consider just a couple of recent examples. In 2013, conservative activists in Texas succeeded in getting the state to discontinue an initiative that was created by 20 regional Texas Educational Service Centers and used in almost 900 schools because of concerns that the content "promoted a progressive pro-Islamic curriculum" that was anti-American. See Rebecca Klein, "Texas Ends CSCOPE Curriculum System after Concerns That It Had an Anti-American Agenda," *Huffington Post*, May 21, 2013. Accessed at: http://www.huffingtonpost.com/2013/05/21/texas-ends-cscope_n_3308963.html (July 1, 2014). In Louisiana, public schools continue to fight what has become a perennial battle over how to present evolution and creationism. See Valerie Strauss, "High School Senior Leads Louisiana Fight against Anti-Evolution Law," *Washington Post*, April 22, 2011. Accessed at: http://www.washingtonpost.com/blogs/answer-sheet/post/high-school-senior-leads-louisiana-fight-against-anti-evolution-law/2011/04/21/AFs8M4LE_blog.html (July 1, 2014).

14. For information about the history and programs of the Peace Corps, visit the organization's website: http://www.peacecorps.gov/about/.

15. For information about the history and programs of AmeriCorps, visit the organization's website: http://www.nationalservice.gov/programs/americorps.

16. For information about the history and programs of Teach for America, visit the organization's website: http://www.teachforamerica.org/our-organization.

17. For information about these organizations' missions, programs, and reach, visit their websites: Envision: http://www.envisionexperience.com; Hugh O'Brien Youth Leadership Foundation: http://www.hoby.org/; Youth to Leaders / Tavis Smiley Foundation: http://www.youthtoleaders.org/home.html; Youth Leadership Institute: http://www.yli.org/; National Youth Leadership Council: http://nylc.org.

18. During their annual conference of high school students, Boys State and Girls State run mock US Senate elections and simulate the legislative process. For a full description of their programs, see: http://www.legion.org/boysnation/about.

19. For the famous *Schoolhouse Rock* "I'm Just a Bill" video, see: http://www.schoolhouserocklive.net/synopsis/ (July 7, 2014).

20. For more on the Third Way, visit the organization's website: http://www.thirdway.org/about_us.

21. For more on Main Street Advocacy, visit the organization's website: http://msa.baskdigital.com/about/.

22. Martha Irvine, "Survey: 97 Percent of Children Play Video Games," *Huffington Post*, September 16, 2008. Accessed at: http://www.huffingtonpost.com/2008/09/16/survey-97-percent-of-chil_n_126948.html (June 24, 2014).

23. "Daily Media Use among Children and Teens Up Dramatically from Five Years Ago," *Kaiser Family Foundation*, January 20, 2010. Accessed at: http:// kff.org/disparities-policy/press-release/daily-media-use-among-children-and-teens-up-dramatically-from-five-years-ago/ (June 22, 2014).

24. For a summary of the National Survey of Student Engagement data from first year-college students, see James Cole, "First-year students reported use of video games and social media in high school: Should we be concerned?" Presented at the 31st Annual Conference on the First-Year Experience, February 2012. Accessed at: http://cpr.iub.edu/uploads/2012_FYE_Video%20 Games.pdf (June 22, 2014).

25. Amanda Lenhart, Joseph Kahne, Ellen Middaugh, Alexander Middaugh, Alexandra MacGill, Chris Evans, and Jessica Vitak, "Teens, Video Games, and Civics," *Pew Research Internet Project*, September 16, 2008. Accessed at: http://www.pewinternet.org/2008/09/16/teens-video-games-and-civics/ (August 31, 2014).

26. Steven Johnson, "SimCandidate: Video games simulate sports, business, and war. Why not politics?" *Slate.com*, December 16, 2003. Accessed at: http:// www.slate.com/articles/technology/webhead/2003/12/simcandidate.html (July 18, 2014).

27. For lists of the top political video games, see "Top Ten Political Videos," *gamemoir.com*, February 17, 2014. Accessed at: http://gamemoir.com/2014/ 02/17/top-ten-political-video-games/ (July 18, 2014); and *GamePolitics.com*, April 9, 2014. Accessed at: http://www.gamepolitics.com/category/topics/ games-about-politics#.U8ytDMJOWzc. (July 18, 2014).

28. Jane Harman, "My Bright Idea: Jane Harman on Using Games to Fix Government," *Wilson Center*, August 23, 2012. Accessed at: http://www. wilsoncenter.org/article/my-bright-idea-jane-harman-using-games-to-fix-government (June 23, 2014).

29. To read about and play the redistricting game, visit the Annenberg School's game website: http://redistrictinggame.org/index.php?pg=about.

30. According to data from the US Department of Health and Human Services, approximately 54 percent of people under the age of 25 have tried marijuana. See Paul Armentano, "Marijuana Use by the Numbers," *NORML*, September 10, 2009. Accessed at: http://blog.norml.org/2009/09/10/marijuana-use-by-the-numbers/ (July 14, 2014).

31. For a contemporary description of the college admission process, see the National Association for College Admission Counseling's website: http:// www.nacacnet.org/Pages/default.aspx.

32. A 2007 survey of 18–24 year olds found that only 37 percent could locate Iraq on a map, even though the United States had been fighting a war in the country for four years. For a summary and analysis of young people's dismal levels of political awareness, see Lory Hough, "Don't Know Much

about Geography," *Harvard Graduate School of Education*. Accessed at: http://www.gse.harvard.edu/news_events/ed/2007/winter/features/geography.html (June 28, 2014).

33. "75% of Oklahoma High School Students Can't Name the First President of the U.S.," *News9.com*, September 16, 2009. Accessed at: http://www.news9.com/story/11141949/75-percent-of-oklahoma-high-school-students-cant-name-the-first-president-of-the-us (August 29, 2014). For more on what high school and college students do and do not know, see, for example, Tamar Lewin, "Average Scores Slip on SATs," *New York Times*, September 15, 2011. Accessed at: http://www.nytimes.com/2011/09/15/education/15sat.html?ref=us&_r=0 (July 2, 2014); and Sandy Hingston, "Is It Just Us, or Are Kids Getting Really Stupid?" *Philadelphia Magazine*, November 26, 2010. Accessed at: http://www.phillymag.com/articles/feature-is-it-just-us-or-are-kids-getting-really-stupid/ (July 2, 2014).

34. Karlos Barrio Marcelos, "Volunteering among High School Students," *Center for Information & Research on Civic Learning & Engagement*, July 2007. Accessed at: http://www.civicyouth.org/PopUps/FactSheets/FS07_High_School_Volunteering.pdf (June 28, 2014).

35. The website is careful to urge young people to do volunteer work for causes they support, but the message is clear that these activities will strengthen their college applications. See "Can Volunteer Work Help You Get into College?" *My College Guide*. Accessed at: http://mycollegeguide.org/blog/11/2011/volunteer-work-college/ (June 30, 2014).

36. The full report can be accessed and downloaded at http://www.american.edu/spa/wpi/upload/Girls-Just-Wanna-Not-Run_Policy-Report.pdf (July 2, 2014).

37. For details about IGNITE's programs and outcomes, visit the organization's website: http://ignitenational.org/.

38. For details about Running Start, visit the organization's website: http://runningstartonline.org/.

39. For similar findings among adult potential candidates, see Fox and Lawless 2011b.

40. "How Young People Use Mobiles: Top Seven Statistics from the Mobile Youth Report." Accessed at: http://mobilesocialwork.wordpress.com/2013/07/25/how-young-people-use-mobiles-top-7-statistics-from-the-mobile-youth-report/ (June 22, 2014).

41. Sheldon G. Adelson, Warren E. Buffet, and Bill Gates, "Break the Immigration Impasse," *New York Times*, July 10, 2014. Accessed at: http://www.nytimes.com/2014/07/11/opinion/sheldon-adelson-warren-buffett-and-bill-gates-on-immigration-reform.html (July 17, 2014).

WORKS CITED

Aamidor, Abe, Jim A. Kuypers, and Susan Wiesinger. 2013. *Media Smackdown: Deconstructing the News and the Future of Journalism*. New York: Peter Lang.

Abramowitz, Alan I. 1988. "Explaining Senate Election Outcomes." *American Political Science Review* 82(2):385–403.

———. 1991. "Incumbency, Campaign Spending, and the Decline of Competition in U.S. House Elections." *Journal of Politics* 53(1):34–56.

———. 2012. "Grand Old Tea Party: Partisan Polarization and the Rise of the Tea Party Movement." In *Steep: The Precipitous Rise of the Tea Party*, eds. Lawrence Rosenthal and Christine Trost. Oakland: University of California Press.

Ahn, T.K., Robert Huckfeldt, and John Barry Ryan. 2010. "Communication, Influence, and Informational Asymmetries among Voters." *Political Psychology* 31:763–87.

Ahuja, Sunil. 2008. *Congress Behaving Badly: The Rise of Partisanship and Incivility and the Death of Public Trust*. Westport, CT: Praeger Publishers.

Aldrich, John H., Bradford H. Bishop, Rebecca S. Hatch, D. Sunshine Hillygus, and David W. Rohde. 2014. "Blame, Responsibility, and the Tea Party in the 2010 Midterm Elections." *Political Behavior* 36:471–91.

Alford, John, Carolyn L. Funk, and John R. Hibbing. 2005. "Are Political Orientations Genetically Transmitted?" *American Political Science Review* 99(2): 153–67.

———, ———, and ———. 2008. "Twin Studies, Molecular Genetics, Politics, and Tolerance: A Response to Beckwith and Morris." *Perspectives on Politics* 6(4):793–7.

Almond, Gabriel Abraham and Sidney Verba. 1963. *The Civic Culture: Political Attitudes and Democracy in Five Nations*. Princeton: Princeton University Press.

Anderson, Peter J., Michael Williams, and George Ogola, eds. 2013. *The Future of Quality News Journalism: A Cross-Continental Analysis*. New York: Routledge.

Andolina, Molly W., Krista Jenkins, Cliff Zukin, and Scott Keeter. 2003. "Habits from Home, Lessons from School: Influences on Youth Civic Engagement." *PS: Political Science & Politics* 36(2):275–80.

Ashby, Julie S. and Ingrid Schoon. 2010. "Career Success: The Role of Teenage Career Aspirations, Ambition Value and Gender in Predicting Adult Social Status and Earnings." *Journal of Vocational Behavior* 77(3):350–60.

Bafumi, Joseph and Michael C. Herron. 2010. "Leapfrog Representation and Extremism: A Study of American Voters and Their Members in Congress." *American Political Science Review* 104(3):519–42.

Banaji, Shakuntala and David Buckingham. 2010. "Young People, the Internet, and Civic Participation: An Overview of Key Findings from the Civicweb Project." *International Journal of Learning and Media* 2(1):1–10.

Barabas, Jason and Jennifer Jerit. 2009. "Estimating the Causal Effects of Media Coverage on Policy-Specific Knowledge." *American Journal of Political Science* 53(1):73–89.

Barber, Michael and Nolan McCarty. 2013. "Causes and Consequences of Polarization." In *Negotiating Agreement in Politics*, eds. Cathie Jo Martin and Jane Mansbridge. Washington, DC: American Political Science Association.

Basinger, Scott. 2013. "Scandals and Congressional Elections in the Post-Watergate Era." *Political Research Quarterly* 66(2):385–98.

Bass, Bernard M. and Ruth Bass. 2008. *The Bass Handbook of Leadership: Theory, Research, and Managerial Applications*, 4th edition. New York: Free Press.

Bauerlein, Mark. 2008. *The Dumbest Generation: How the Digital Age Stupefies Young Americans and Jeopardizes Our Future (Or, Don't Trust Anyone Under 30)*. New York: Penguin.

Baum, Matthew A. and Tim Groeling. 2008. "New Media and the Polarization of American Political Discourse." *Political Communication* 25(4):345–65.

Beck, Paul Allen and M. Kent Jennings. 1982. "Pathways to Participation." *American Political Science Review* 76(1):94–108.

Bennett, W. Lance. 2002. *News: The Politics of Illusion*, 5th edition. New York: Longman.

———. 2007. *Civic Life Online: Learning How Digital Media Can Engage Youth*. Cambridge, MA: MIT Press.

———. 2008. "Changing Citizenship in the Digital Age." In *Civic Life Online: Learning How Digital Media Can Engage Youth*, ed. W. Lance Bennett. Cambridge, MA: MIT Press.

Bennett, W. Lance and Alexandra Segerberg. 2014. *The Logic of Connective Action: Digital Media and the Personalization of Contentious Politics*. New York: Cambridge University Press.

Billig, Shelley, Sue Root, and Dan Jesse. 2005. "The Impact of Participation in Service-Learning on High School Students' Civic Engagement." College Park, MD: Center for Information and Research on Civic Learning and Engagement.

Binder, Sarah A. 1999. "The Dynamics of Legislative Gridlock, 1947–96." *American Political Science Review* 93(3):519–33.

———. 2003. *Stalemate: Causes and Consequences of Legislative Gridlock.* Washington, DC: Brookings Institution Press.

Black, Gordon S. 1972. "A Theory of Political Ambition: Career Choices and the Role of Structural Incentives." *American Political Science Review* 66(1):144–59.

Borah, Porismita. 2014. "Does It Matter Where You Read the News Story? Interaction of Incivility and News Frames in the Political Blogosphere." *Communication Research* 41(6):809–27.

Bowler, Shaun and Jeffrey A. Karp. 2004. "Politicians, Scandals, and Trust in Government." *Political Behavior* 26(3):271–87.

Brock, George. 2013. *Out of Print: Newspapers, Journalism and the Business of News in the Digital Age.* London: Kogan Page Publishers.

Brown, Sarah, Aurora Ortiz-Nuñez, and Karl Taylor. 2001. "What Will I Be When I Grow Up? An Analysis of Childhood Expectations and Career Outcomes." *Economics of Education Review* 30(3):493–506.

Buell, Emmett H., Jr. and Lee Sigelman. 2008. *Attack Politics: Negativity in Presidential Campaigns since 1960.* Lawrence: University Press of Kansas.

Burns, Nancy, Kay Lehman Schlozman, and Sidney Verba. 2001. *The Private Roots of Public Action: Gender, Equality, and Political Participation.* Cambridge, MA: Harvard University Press.

Campbell, David E. 2008. "Voice in the Classroom: How an Open Classroom Climate Fosters Political Engagement among Adolescents." *Political Behavior* 30(4):437–54.

Campbell, Sean. 2006. *The Sitcoms of Norman Lear.* Jefferson, NC: McFarland.

Canon, David T. 1993. "Sacrificial Lambs or Strategic Politicians? Political Amateurs in the US Elections." *American Journal of Political Science* 37(4):1119–41.

———. 1999. *Race, Redistricting, and Representation: The Unintended Consequences of Black Majority Districts.* Chicago: University of Chicago Press.

Carson, Jamie L., Michael H. Crespin, Charles J. Finocchiaro, and David W. Rohde. 2007. "Redistricting and Party Polarization in the U.S. House of Representatives." *American Politics Research* 35(6):878–90.

Castells, Manuel. 2012. *Networks of Outrage and Hope: Social Networks in the Internet Age.* Berkeley: University of California Press.

Charney, Evan and William English. 2012. "Candidate Genes and Political Behavior." *American Political Science Review* 106(1):1–34.

Clarke, Harold D., Frank B. Feigert, Barry J. Seldon, and Marianne C. Stewart. 1999. "More Time with My Money: Leaving the House and Going Home in 1992 and 1994." *Political Research Quarterly* 52(1):67–85.

Cogburn, Derrick L. and Fatima K. Espinoza-Vasquez. 2011. "From Networked Nominee to Networked Nation: Examining the Impact of Web 2.0 and Social Media on Political Participation and Civic Engagement in the 2008 Obama Campaign." *Journal of Political Marketing* 10(1–2):189–213.

Cohen, Cathy J. and Michael C. Dawson. 1993. "Neighborhood Poverty and African American Politics." *American Political Science Review* 87(2):286–302.

Cohen, Cathy J., Joseph Kahne, Benjamin Bowyer, Ellen Middaugh, and Jon Rogowski. 2012. *Participatory Politics: New Media and Youth Political Action.* Oakland, CA: YPP Research Network, Mills College School of Education.

Conger, Jay A. and Ronald E. Riggio, eds. 2007. *The Practice of Leadership: Developing the Next Generation of Leaders.* San Francisco: Jossey-Bass.

Conway, M. Margaret. 1991. *Political Participation in the United States,* 2nd edition. Washington, DC: Congressional Quarterly Press.

Cook, Timothy E. 1998. *Governing with the News: The News Media as a Political Institution.* Chicago: University of Chicago Press.

Cook, Timothy E. and Paul Gronke. 2005. "The Skeptical American: Revisiting the Meanings of Trust in Government and Confidence in Institutions." *Journal of Politics* 67(3):784–803.

Cowley, Philip. 2002. *Revolts & Rebellions: Parliamentary Voting Under Blair.* London: Politico.

Cox, Gary W. and Jonathan N. Katz. 1996. "Why Did the Incumbency Advantage in US House Elections Grow?" *American Journal of Political Science* 40(2): 478–97.

Cronin, Thomas E. and Michael A. Genovese. 2012. *Leadership Matters: Unleashing the Power of Paradox.* Boulder, CO: Paradigm.

Dalton, Mary M. and Laura R. Linder. 2012. *The Sitcom Reader: America Viewed and Skewed.* Albany: State University of New York Press.

Dalton, Russell. 2008. *The Good Citizen: How a Younger Generation Is Reshaping American Politics.* Washington, DC: Congressional Quarterly Press.

Damon, William. 2011. *Failing Liberty 101: How We Are Leaving Young Americans Unprepared for Citizenship in a Free Society.* Stanford, CA: Hoover Institution Press.

Dancey, Logan. 2012. "The Consequences of Political Cynicism: How Cynicism Shapes Citizens' Reactions to Political Scandals." *Political Behavior* 34(3): 411–23.

Davis, Richard. 2009. *Typing Politics: The Role of Blogs in American Politics.* New York: Oxford University Press.

Delli Carpini, Michael X. and Scott Keeter. 1996. *What Americans Know about Politics and Why It Matters.* New Haven, CT: Yale University Press.

Dines, Gail and Jean M. Humez. 2014. *Gender, Race, and Class in Media,* 4th edition. Los Angeles: Sage.

Dionne, E. J. 2013. *Why Americans Hate Politics.* New York: Simon and Schuster.

Dow, Bonnie. 2001. "Ellen, Television, and the Politics of Gay and Lesbian Visibility." *Critical Studies in Media Communication* 18(2):123–40.

Draper, Robert. 2012. *Do Not Ask What Good We Do: Inside the US House of Representatives.* New York: Simon and Schuster.

Dubrin, Andrew J. 2012. *Leadership: Research Findings, Practice, and Skills,* 7th edition. Independence, KY: Cengage Learning.

Edwards, Mickey. 2012. *The Parties Versus the People: How to Turn Republicans and Democrats into Americans*. New Haven, CT: Yale University Press.

Elder, Laurel. 2004. "Why Women Don't Run." *Women & Politics* 26(2):27–56.

Erikson, Robert S. and Laura Stoker. 2011. "Caught in the Draft: The Effects of Vietnam Draft Lottery Status on Political Attitudes." *American Political Science Review* 105(2):221–37.

Fiorina, Morris. 1981. *Retrospective Voting in American National Elections*. New Haven, CT: Yale University Press.

Flanagan, Constance and Peter Levine. 2010. "Civic Engagement and the Transition to Adulthood." *Future of Children* 20(1):159–79.

Fowler, James H., Laura A. Baker, and Christopher T. Dawes. 2008. "Genetic Variation in Political Participation." *American Political Science Review* 102(2):233–48.

Fox, Richard L. and Jennifer L. Lawless. 2011a. "Gains and Losses in Interest in Running for Office: The Concept of Dynamic Political Ambition." *Journal of Politics* 73(2):443–62.

———— and ————. 2011b. "Gendered Perceptions and Political Candidacies: A Central Barrier to Women's Equality in Electoral Politics." *American Journal of Political Science* 55(1):59–73.

———— and ————. 2014. "Uncovering the Origins of the Gender Gap in Political Ambition." *American Political Science Review* 108(3):499–519.

Fulton, Sarah A., Cherie D. Maestas, L. Sandy Maisel, and Walter J. Stone. 2006. "The Sense of a Woman: Gender, Ambition and the Decision to Run for Congress." *Political Research Quarterly* 59(2):235–48.

Funk, Carolyn L. 1996. "The Impact of Scandal on Candidate Evaluations: An Experimental Test of the Role of Candidate Traits." *Political Behavior* 18(1):1–24.

Gaddie, Ronald Keith. 2004. *Born to Run: Origins of the Political Career*. Lanham, MD: Rowman and Littlefield.

Galston, William A. 2007. "Civic Knowledge, Civic Education, and Civic Engagement: A Summary of Recent Research." *International Journal of Public Administration* 30(6–7):623–42.

————. 2001. "Political Knowledge, Political Engagement, and Civic Education." *Annual Review of Political Science* 4:217–34.

Gamble, Katrina L. 2007. "Black Political Representation: An Examination of Legislative Activity within US House Committees." *Legislative Studies Quarterly* 32(3):421–47.

Gartner, Scott Sigmund and Gary M. Segura. 2008. "All Politics are Still Local: The Iraq War and the 2006 Midterm Elections." *PS: Political Science & Politics* 41(1):95–100.

Geer, John G. 2006. *In Defense Of Negativity: Attack Ads in Presidential Campaigns*. Chicago: University of Chicago Press.

————. 2012. "The News Media and the Rise of Negativity in Presidential Campaigns." *PS: Political Science and Politics* 45(3):422–7.

————. 2013. "The News Media and the Rise of Negativity in Presidential Campaigns: A New Hypothesis." In *Can We Talk? The Rise of Rude, Nasty, Stubborn Politics*, eds. Daniel M. Shea and Morris P. Fiorina. New York: Pearson.

Gerbaudo, Paulo. 2012. *Tweets and the Streets: Social Media and Contemporary Activism*. New York: Pluto Press.

Gilmour, John B. 1995. *Strategic Disagreement: Stalemate in American Politics*. Pittsburgh: University of Pittsburgh Press.

Glanville, Jennifer L. 1999. "Political Socialization or Selection? Adolescent Extracurricular Participation and Political Activity in Early Adulthood." *Social Science Quarterly* 80(2):279–90.

Goidel, Kirby. 2013. *America's Failing Experiment: How We the People Have Become the Problem*. Lanham, MD: Rowman and Littlefield.

Griffin, John D. and Brian Newman. 2007. "The Unequal Representation of Latinos and Whites." *Journal of Politics* 69(4):1032–46.

Grose, Christian R. 2005. "Disentangling Constituency and Legislator Effects in Representation: Black Legislators or Black Districts?" *Social Science Quarterly* 86(2):427–43.

Grover, Steven L. and Marcus C. Hasel. 2014. "How Leaders Recover (or Not) from Publicized Sex Scandals." *Journal of Business Ethics*: DOI: 10.1007/s10551-014-2146-3.

Hart, Daniel, Thomas M. Donnelly, James Youniss, and Robert Atkins. 2007. "High School Community Service as a Predictor of Adult Voting and Volunteering." *American Education Research Journal* 44(1):197–219.

Hayes, Danny. 2011. "When Gender and Party Collide: Stereotyping in Candidate Trait Attribution." *Politics & Gender* 7(2):133–65.

Hayes, Danny and Jennifer L. Lawless. 2015. "A Non-Gendered Lens? Media, Voters, and Female Candidates in Contemporary Congressional Elections." *Perspectives on Politics* 13(1):forthcoming.

Healy, Andrew and Neil Malhotra. 2010. "Random Events, Economic Losses, and Retrospective Voting: Implications for Democratic Competence." *Quarterly Journal of Political Science* 5(2):193–208.

Hendricks, John Allen and Robert E. Denton, Jr. 2010. "Political Campaigns and Communicating with the Electorate in the Twenty-First Century." In *Communicator-in-Chief: How Barack Obama Used New Media Technology to Win the White House*, eds. John Allen Hendricks and Robert E. Denton, Jr. Lanham, MD: Lexington Books.

Hennessy, Cari Lynn and Paul Martin. 2006. "Blogs, the Mainstream Media, and the War in Iraq." Paper presented at the annual meeting for the American Political Science Association: Philadelphia, PA: August 31–September 3.

Herrnson, Paul and James M. Curry. 2011. "Issue Voting and Partisan Defections in Congressional Elections." *Legislative Studies Quarterly* 36(2): 281–307.

Hess, Robert D., Judith Torney-Purta, and Jaan Valsiner. 2006. *The Development of Political Attitudes in Children*. Edison, NJ: Transaction Publishers.

Hetherington, Marc J. 1999. "The Effect of Political Trust on the Presidential Vote, 1968–96." *American Political Science Review* 93(2):311–26.

———. 2005. *Why Trust Matters: Declining Political Trust and the Demise of American Liberalism*. Princeton: Princeton University Press.

Hibbing, John and Elizabeth Theiss-Morse. 2002. *Stealth Democracy: Americans' Beliefs about How Government Should Work*. New York: Cambridge University Press.

Hillygus, D. Sunshine. 2005. "The Missing Link: Exploring the Relationship between Higher Education and Political Engagement." *Political Behavior* 27(1):25–47.

Hirlinger, Michael W. 1992. "Citizen-Initiated Contacting of Local Government Officials: A Multivariate Explanation." *Journal of Politics* 54(2):553–64.

Holbert, Lance R., Dhavan V. Shah, and Nojin Kwak. 2003. "Political Implications of Prime-Time Drama and Sitcom Use: Genres of Representation and Opinions Concerning Women's Rights." *Journal of Communication* 53(1):45–60.

Holbrook, Thomas M., Clayton Clouse, and Aaron C. Weinschenk. 2012. "Bringing the President Back In: The Collapse of Lehman Brothers and the Evolution of Retrospective Voting in the 2008 Presidential Election." *Political Research Quarterly* 65(2):263–74.

Huckfeldt, Robert and Jeanette M. Mendez. 2008. "Moths, Flames, and Political Engagement: Managing Disagreement within Communication Networks." *Journal of Politics* 70(1):83–96.

Iyengar, Shanto and Simon Jackman. 2004. "Technology and Politics: Incentives for Youth Participation." CIRCLE Working Paper No. 24. College Park, MD: Center for Information and Research on Civic Learning and Engagement.

Jacobson, Gary C. 2012. *The Politics of Congressional Elections*, 8th edition. New York: Pearson.

Jamieson, Kathleen Hall and Erika Falk. 2000. "Continuity and Change in Civility in the House." In *Polarized Politics: Congress and the President in a Partisan Era*, eds. Jon R. Bond and Richard Fleisher. Washington, DC: Congressional Quarterly Press.

Jennings, M. Kent. 2002. "Generation Units and the Student Protest Movement in the United States: An Intra- and Intergenerational Analysis." *Political Psychology* 23(2):303–24.

———. 2007. "Political Socialization." In *The Oxford Handbook of Political Behavior*, eds. Russell J. Dalton and Hans-Dieter Klingemann. New York: Oxford University Press.

Jennings, M. Kent and Gregory B. Markus. 1984. "Partisan Orientations over the Long Haul: Results from the Three-Wave Political Socialization Panel Study." *American Political Science Review* 78(4):1000–18.

Jennings, M. Kent and Richard G. Niemi. 1968. "The Transmission of Political Values from Parent to Child." *American Political Science Review* 62(1): 169–84.

——— and ———. 1981. *Generations and Politics: A Panel Study of Young Adults and Their Parents.* Princeton, NJ: Princeton University.

Jennings, M. Kent and Laura Stoker. 2012. "Continuities in Political Participation across Generations." Unpublished manuscript.

Jennings, M. Kent, Laura Stoker, and Jake Bowers. 2009. "Politics across Generations: Family Transmission Reexamined." *Journal of Politics* 71(3):782–99.

Jerit, Jennifer, Jason Barabas, and Toby Bolsen. 2006. "Citizens, Knowledge, and the Information Environment." *American Journal of Political Science* 50(2): 266–82.

Jones, David R. 2001. "Party Polarization and Legislative Gridlock." *Political Research Quarterly* 54(1):125–41.

Kazee, Thomas A. 1994. "The Emergence of Congressional Candidates." In *Who Runs for Congress? Ambition, Context, and Candidate Emergence*, ed. Thomas Kazee. Washington, DC: Congressional Quarterly Press.

Keele, Luke. 2005. "The Authorities Really Do Matter: Party Control and Trust in Government." *Journal of Politics* 67(3):873–86.

Keeter, Scott, Juliana Horowitz, and Alec Tyson. 2008. "Young Voters in the 2008 Election." Washington, DC: Pew Research Center. Accessed at: http://www.pewresearch.org/2008/11/13/young-voters-in-the-2008-election/ (December 12, 2014).

Kerbel, Matthew and Joel D. Bloom. 2005. "Blog for America and Civic Involvement." *Harvard International Journal of Press/Politics* 10(4):3–27.

Kinder, Donald R. 1986. "Presidential Character Revisited." In *Political Cognition*, eds. Richard R. Lau and David O. Sears. Hillsdale, NJ: Erlbaum.

King, David C. 1997. "The Polarization of American Parties and the Mistrust of Government." In *Why People Don't Trust Government*, eds. Joseph S. Nye, Jr., Philip D. Zelikow, and David C. King. Cambridge, MA: Harvard University Press.

Kirkpatrick, Shelley A. and Edwin A. Locke. 1991. "Leadership: Do Traits Matter?" *Academy of Management Executive*, May, 48–60.

Kirlin, Mary. 2003. "The Role of Adolescent Extracurricular Activities in Adult Political Participation." College Park, MD: Center for Information and Research on Civic Learning and Engagement.

Ladd, Jonathan. 2012. *Why Americans Hate the Media and How It Matters.* Princeton, NJ: Princeton University Press.

Larcinese, Valentino. 2007. "Does Political Knowledge Increase Turnout? Evidence from the 1997 British General Election." *Public Choice* 131(3–4):387–411.

Larson, Edward J. 2007. *A Magnificent Catastrophe: The Tumultuous Election of 1800, America's First Presidential Campaign.* New York: Simon & Schuster.

Lau, Richard R. and Ivy Brown Rovner. 2009. "Negative Campaigning." *Annual Review of Political Science* 12:285–306.

Lawless, Jennifer L. 2012. *Becoming a Candidate: Political Ambition and the Decision to Run for Office.* New York: Cambridge University Press.

Lawless, Jennifer L. and Richard L. Fox. 2005. *It Takes a Candidate: Why Women Don't Run for Office.* New York: Cambridge University Press.

——— and ———. 2010. *It Still Takes a Candidate: Why Women Don't Run for Office.* New York: Cambridge University Press.

Lee, Frances E. 2009. *Beyond Ideology: Politics, Principles, and Partisanship in the U.S. Senate.* Chicago: University of Chicago Press.

Leighley, Jan. 1991. "Participation as a Stimulus of Political Conceptualization." *Journal of Politics* 53(1):198–211.

Lord, Robert G., Christy L. de Vader, and George M. Allinger. 1986. "A Meta-Analysis of the Relation between Personality Traits and Leadership Perceptions: An Application of Validity Generalization Procedures." *Journal of Applied Psychology* 71(3):402–10.

Maestas, Cherie. 2003. "The Incentive to Listen: Progressive Ambition, Resources, and Opinion Monitoring among State Legislators." *Journal of Politics* 65(2):439–56.

———. 2000. "Professional Legislatures and Ambitious Politicians: Policy Responsiveness of Individuals and Institutions." *Legislative Studies Quarterly* 25(4):663–90.

Maestas, Cherie, Lonna R. Atkeson, Thomas Croom, and Lisa A. Bryant. 2008. "Shifting the Blame: Federalism, Media, and Public Assignment of Blame Following Hurricane Katrina." *Publius: The Journal of Federalism* 38(4):609–32.

Maestas, Cherie D., Sarah Fulton, L. Sandy Maisel, and Walter J. Stone. 2006. "When to Risk It? Institutions, Ambitions, and the Decision to Run for the U.S. House." *American Political Science Review* 100(2):195–208.

Mann, Thomas E. and Norman J. Ornstein. 2013. *It's Even Worse Than It Looks: How the American Constitutional System Collided with the New Politics of Extremism.* New York: Basic Books.

Mansbridge, Jane. 1999. "Should Blacks Represent Blacks and Women Represent Women? A Contingent 'Yes'." *Journal of Politics* 61(3):628–57.

Markus, Gregory B. 1982. "Political Attitudes during an Election Year: A Report on the 1980 NES Panel Study." *American Political Science Review* 76(3):538–60.

———. 1986. "Stability and Change in Political Attitudes: Observed, Recalled, and Explained." *Political Behavior* 8(1):21–44.

Martin, Aaron J. 2012. *Young People and Politics: Political Engagement in the Anglo-American Democracies.* London: Routledge.

McCarty, Nolan. 2007. "The Policy Effects of Political Polarization." In *The Transformation of American Politics: Activist Government and the Rise of*

Conservatism, eds. Paul Pierson and Theda Skocpol. Princeton, NJ: Princeton University Press.

McFarland, Daniel A. and Reuben J. Thomas. 2006. "Bowling Young: How Youth Voluntary Associations Influence Adult Political Participation." *American Sociological Review* 71(3):401–25.

McIntosh, Hugh, Daniel Hart, and James Youniss. 2007. "The Influence of Family Political Discussion on Youth Civic Development: Which Parent Qualities Matter?" *PS: Political Science & Politics* 40(3):495–9.

McNair, Brian. 2000. *Journalism and Democracy: An Evaluation of the Political Public Square*. New York: Routledge.

Mello, Zena R. 2008. "Gender Variation in Developmental Trajectories of Educational and Occupational Expectations and Attainment from Adolescence to Adulthood." *Developmental Psychology* 44(4):1069–80.

Milner, Henry. 2010. *The Internet Generation: Engaged Citizens or Political Dropouts*. Lebanon, NH: Tufts University Press.

Mindich, David T.Z. 2004. *Tuned Out: Why Americans Under 40 Don't Follow the News*. New York: Oxford University Press.

Minta, Michael. 2009. "Legislative Oversight and Substantive Representation of Black and Latino Interests in Congress." *Legislative Studies Quarterly* 34(2): 193–218.

Montgomery, Kathleen, Barbara Gottlieb-Robles, and Gary Larson. 2004. "Youth as E-Citizens: Engaging the Digital Generation." Washington, DC: Center for Social Media, American University.

Myrdal, Alva. 1941. *Nation and Family*. Cambridge: Massachusetts Institute of Technology.

Nicholson, Stephen P. 2003. "The Political Environment and Ballot Proposition Awareness." *American Journal of Political Science* 47(3):403–10.

Niemi, Richard G. 1974. *How Family Members Perceive Each Other; Political and Social Attitudes in Two Generations*. New Haven, CT: Yale University Press.

Niemi, Richard and Mary Hepburn. 1995. "The Rebirth of Political Socialization." *Perspectives on Political Science* 24(1):7–16.

Niemi, Richard G. and Jane Junn. 1998. *Civic Education: What Makes Students Learn*. New Haven, CT: Yale University Press.

Northouse, Peter G. 2012. *Leadership: Theory and Practice*, 6th edition. Thousand Oaks, CA: Sage.

Nye, Joseph S., Jr, Philip Zelikow, and David C. King, eds. 1997. *Why People Don't Trust Government*. Cambridge, MA: Harvard University Press.

Nyhan, Brendan. 2014. "Scandal Potential: How Political Context and News Congestion Affect the President's Vulnerability to Media Scandal." *British Journal of Political Science*: forthcoming.

Owen, Diana and Jack Dennis. 1988. "Gender Differences in the Politicization of American Children." *Women & Politics* 8(3):23–43.

Panagopoulos, Costas and Peter L. Francia. 2009. "Grassroots Mobilization in the 2008 Presidential Election." *Journal of Political Marketing* 8(4):315–33.

Pasek, Josh, Lauren Feldman, Daniel Romer, and Kathleen Hall Jamieson. 2008. "Schools as Incubators of Democratic Participation: Building Long-Term Political Efficacy with Civic Education." *Applied Developmental Science* 12(1): 26–37.

Patterson, Thomas. 2013. *Informing the News.* New York: Vintage.

Piven, Frances Fox and Richard A. Cloward. 1997. *The Breaking of the American Social Compact.* New York: New Press.

Preuhs, Robert R. 2006. "The Conditional Effects of Minority Descriptive Representation: Black Legislators and Policy Influence in the American States." *Journal of Politics* 68(3):585–99.

Prinz, Timothy S. 1993. "The Career Paths of Elected Politicians: A Review and Prospectus." In *Ambition and Beyond: Career Paths of American Politicians*, eds. S. Williams and E. Lascher. Berkeley, CA: Institute of Governmental Studies.

Prior, Markus. 2005. "News v. Entertainment: How Increasing Media Choice Widens Gaps in Political Knowledge and Turnout." *American Journal of Political Science* 49(3):577–92.

———. 2007. *Post-Broadcast Democracy: How Media Choice Increases Inequality in Political Involvement and Polarizes Elections.* New York: Cambridge University Press.

Rahn, Wendy M., John H. Aldrich, Eugene Borgida, and John L. Sullivan. 1990. "A Social Cognitive Model of Candidate Appraisal." In *Information and Democratic Processes*, eds. John A. Ferejohn and James H. Kuklinski. Urbana: University of Illinois Press.

Renshon, Stanley Allen. 1974. *Psychological Needs and Political Behavior: A Theory of Personality and Political Efficacy.* New York: Free Press.

Richman, Jesse. 2011. "Parties, Pivots, and Policy: The Status Quo Test." *American Political Science Review* 105(1):151–65.

Ridout, Travis N. and Glen R. Smith. 2008. "Free Advertising: How the Media Amplify Campaign Messages." *Political Research Quarterly* 61(4):598–608.

Rohde, David W. 1979. "Risk-Bearing and Progressive Ambition: The Case of the US House of Representatives." *American Journal of Political Science* 23(1):1–26.

Rosenstone, Steven J. and John Mark Hansen. 1993. *Mobilization, Participation, and Democracy in America.* Ann Arbor: University of Michigan Press.

Rottinghaus, Brandon. 2014. "Monkey Business: The Effect of Scandals on Presidential Primary Nominations." *PS: Political Science & Politics* 47(2):379–85.

Ryan, John Barry. 2011. "Social Networks as a Shortcut to Correct Voting." *American Journal of Political Science* 55(4):753–66.

Sander, Thomas H. and Robert D. Putnam. 2010. "Still Bowling Alone? The Post-9/11 Split." *Journal of Democracy* 21(1):9–16.

Sapiro, Virginia. 2004. "Not Your Parents' Political Socialization: Introduction for a New Generation." *Annual Review of Political Science* 7:1–23.

Schacter, Daniel L. 1999. "The Seven Sins of Memory: Insights from Psychology and Cognitive Neuroscience." *American Psychologist* 54:182–203.

Schacter, Daniel L., Joan Y. Chiao, and Jason P. Mitchell. 2003. "The Seven Sins of Memory: Implications for the Self." In *The Self: From Soul to Brain*, eds. Joseph LeDoux, Jacek Debiece, and Henry Moss. New York: Annals of the New York Academy of Sciences.

Schlesinger, Joseph A. 1966. *Ambition and Politics: Political Careers in the United States*. Chicago: Rand NcNally.

Schneider, Monica and Angela Bos. 2012. "The Interplay of Gender and Party Stereotypes in Evaluating Political Candidates." Presented at the annual meeting of the Western Political Science Association, Portland, OR, March 22–24.

———— and ————. 2013. "Measuring Stereotypes of Female Politicians." *Political Psychology* 35(2):245–66.

Schoon, Ingrid. 2001. "Teenage Job Aspirations and Career Attainment in Adulthood: A 17-Year Follow-Up Study of Teenagers Who Aspired to Become Scientists, Health Professionals, or Engineers." *International Journal of Behavioral Development* 25(2):124–32.

Schoon, Ingrid and Samantha Parsons. 2002. "Teenage Aspirations for Future Careers and Occupational Outcomes." *Journal of Vocational Behavior* 60(2):262–88.

Schoon, Ingrid and Elzbieta Polek. 2011. "Teenage Career Aspirations and Adult Career Attainment: The Role of Gender, Social Background and General Cognitive Ability." *International Journal of Behavioral Development* 35(3): 210–17.

Shirky, Clay. 2009. *Here Comes Everybody: The Power of Organizing without Organizations*. New York: Penguin Books.

Sinclair, Barbara. 2006. *Party Wars: Polarization and the Politics of National Policy Making*. Norman: University of Oklahoma Press.

Skocpol, Theda and Vanessa Williamson. 2012. *The Tea Party and the Remaking of Republican Conservatism*. New York: Oxford University Press.

Soss, Joe. 1999. "Lessons of Welfare: Policy Design, Political Learning, and Political Action." *American Political Science Review* 93(2):363–80.

Squire, Peverill. 1988. "Career Opportunities and Membership Stability in Legislatures." *Legislative Studies Quarterly* 13(1):65–80.

Stogdill, Ralph Melvin. 1974. *Handbook of Leadership: A Survey of Theory and Research*. New York: Free Press.

Stoker, Laura and Jackie Bass. 2011. "Political Socialization: Ongoing Questions and New Directions." In *The Oxford Handbook of American Public Opinion and the Media*, eds. Robert Y. Shapiro and Lawrence R. Jacobs. New York: Oxford University Press.

Stoker, Laura and M. Kent Jennings. 1995. "Life-Cycle Transitions and Political Participation: The Case of Marriage." *American Political Science Review* 89(2):421–33.

Theriault, Sean M. 2008. *Party Polarization in Congress*. New York: Cambridge University Press.

———. 2013. *The Gingrich Senators: The Roots of Partisan Warfare in Congress*. New York: Oxford University Press.

Thomas, Sue. 1998. "Introduction: Women and Elective Office: Past, Present, and Future." In *Women and Elective Office*, eds. Sue Thomas and Clyde Wilcox. New York: Oxford University Press.

Torney-Purta, Judith, Jack Schwille, and Jo-Ann Amadeo. 1999. *Civic Education across Countries: Twenty-Four National Case Studies from the IEA Civic Education Project*. Amsterdam: International Association for the Evaluation of Educational Achievement.

Trice, Ashton D. and Nancy McClellan. 1993. "Do Children's Career Aspirations Predict Adult Occupations? An Answer from a Secondary Analysis of a Longitudinal Study." *Psychological Reports* 72:368–70.

Verba, Sidney, Kay Lehman Schlozman, and Henry E. Brady. 1995. *Voice and Equality: Civic Voluntarism in American Politics*. Cambridge, MA: Harvard University Press.

Verba, Sidney, Kay Lehman Schlozman, and Nancy Burns. 2005. "Family Ties: Understanding the Intergenerational Transmission of Political Participation." In *The Social Logic of Politics*, ed. Alan S. Zuckerman. Philadelphia: Temple University Press.

Wattenberg, Martin P. 2011. *Is Voting for Young People?* Boston: Pearson.

West, Darrell M. 2009. *Air Wars: Television Advertising in Election Campaigns, 1952–2008*, 5th edition. Washington, DC: Congressional Quarterly Press.

Wiesinger, Susan. 2013. *Media Smackdown: Deconstructing the News and the Future of Journalism*. New York: Peter Lang.

Williamson, Vanessa, Theda Skocpol, and John Coggin. 2011. "The Tea Party and the Remaking of Republican Conservatism." *Perspectives on Politics* 9(1):25–43.

Wilson, William J. 1991. "Public Policy Research and the Truly Disadvantaged." In *The Urban Underclass*, eds. Christopher Jencks and Paul E. Peterson. Washington, DC: Brookings Institution.

Woon, Jonathan. 2012. "Democratic Accountability and Retrospective Voting: A Laboratory Experiment." *American Journal of Political Science* 56(4):913–30.

INDEX